LAWS AND LEGISLATION

CREDIT CARD ACCOUNTABILITY RESPONSIBILITY AND DISCLOSURE ACT

EFFECTS AND PROTECTIONS

LAWS AND LEGISLATION

Additional books in this series can be found on Nova's website under the Series tab.

Additional E-books in this series can be found on Nova's website under the E-book tab.

LAWS AND LEGISLATION

CREDIT CARD ACCOUNTABILITY RESPONSIBILITY AND DISCLOSURE ACT

EFFECTS AND PROTECTIONS

OLIVER P. MEYER
EDITOR

nova publishers
New York

For permission to use material from this book please contact us:
Telephone 631-231-7269; Fax 631-231-8175
Web Site: http://www.novapublishers.com

Additional color graphics may be available in the e-book version of this book.

Library of Congress Cataloging-in-Publication Data

ISBN: 978-1-62948-689-5

Published by Nova Science Publishers, Inc. † New York

Contents

PREFACE

The CARD Act directs the Consumer Financial Protection Bureau to conduct a biennial review of the consumer credit card market, including the effect of the Act on the cost and availability of credit and the adequacy of protections for consumers relating to credit card plans. This book presents the findings of the Bureau's review and the impact of the CARD Act on the marketplace.

Chapter 1 – Prepared Remarks of Richard Cordray, Director of the Consumer Financial Protection Bureau. Hearing on CARD (Credit Card Accountability Responsibility and Disclosure) Act Field.

Chapter 2 – The Credit Card Accountability Responsibility and Disclosure Act of 2009 ("CARD Act" or "the Act") changed the landscape of the credit card market. The CARD Act was enacted to "establish fair and transparent practices related to the extension of credit" in this market, regulating both the underwriting and pricing of credit card accounts. Among other things, the Act prohibits credit card issuers from extending credit without assessing the consumer's ability to pay, with special rules regarding the extension of credit to persons under the age of 21. The Act restricts the amount of "upfront" fees that an issuer can charge during the first year after an account is opened, and limits the instances in which issuers can charge "back-end" penalty fees when a consumer makes a late payment or exceeds his or her credit limit. The Act also restricts the circumstances under which issuers can increase interest rates on credit cards and establishes procedures for doing so.

Implementation of the CARD Act was vested originally with the Board of Governors of the Federal Reserve System ("Board"), and passed to the Consumer Financial Protection Bureau ("CFPB" or "Bureau") on July 21, 2011, pursuant to the Dodd-Frank Wall Street Reform and Consumer

Protection Act ("Dodd-Frank Act"). The CARD Act directs the Bureau to conduct a biennial review of the consumer credit card market, including the effect of the Act on the cost and availability of credit and the adequacy of protections for consumers relating to credit card plans. This is the first such report the Bureau has prepared. The report draws upon publicly and commercially available data as well as data obtained by the Bureau through its supervision of large credit card issuers.*

Based on our analysis of the data, as well as our experience monitoring the credit card market for risks to consumers, we present the following findings.

* The CFPB considers all supervisory information to be confidential. Consistent with the Bureau's rules, the data findings presented in this paper do not directly or indirectly identify the institutions or consumers involved. *See* 12 C.F.R. § 1070.41(c).

In: Credit Card Accountability Responsibility … ISBN: 978-1-62948-689-5
Editor: Oliver P. Meyer

Chapter 1

PREPARED REMARKS OF RICHARD CORDRAY, DIRECTOR OF THE CONSUMER FINANCIAL PROTECTION BUREAU. HEARING ON CARD (CREDIT CARD ACCOUNTABILITY RESPONSIBILITY AND DISCLOSURE) ACT FIELD*

Thank you so much for being here with us today. I am always happy to be back in Chicago, where I spent three good years as a law student. We are hosting this field hearing to discuss the effects of the Credit Card Accountability Responsibility and Disclosure Act, a law commonly known as the CARD Act. The CARD Act was passed with the specific goal of making the credit card market fairer and more transparent for consumers. Today, we are releasing a report that Congress required us to prepare about the impact of the CARD Act on the marketplace.

Before we discuss the results of our report, however, it is important to describe conditions in the marketplace when the CARD Act was signed into law. The economic landscape in May 2009 was quite poor. The housing market had crashed. Unemployment had risen to 9.4 percent. A whopping 14.5 million people were out of work, and that number was expected to continue to grow. Gross domestic product had moved sharply into negative territory,

---

* This is an edited, reformatted and augmented version of testimony Presented October 2, 2013 at the CARD Act Field Hearing in Chicago Illinois.

falling by 8.3 percent and 5.4 percent in the previous two quarters, and the Federal Reserve was predicting it would drop even further.

At that time, I was serving as Ohio's Attorney General, and we saw firsthand how hard people were struggling to stay afloat. Particularly with respect to credit cards, people were extremely frustrated, and they were complaining loudly and frequently about being dinged by unexpected fees and about dealing with card agreements full of fine print and legalese they could not decipher or understand. The bottom line at the time was that consumers had no good way to assess the true cost of their credit card upfront. Some members of Congress became interested in how to address the challenges raised by their constituents, and the Federal Reserve had swung into action and developed some new rules in this area. Against that backdrop, Congress passed the CARD Act to address troublesome practices and reform the credit card markets.

One problem that consumers faced was hidden, excessive, and unfair fees. These fees made it hard for consumers to anticipate costs. In some cases, they could not avoid these fees and did not know they were coming. Maybe a consumer's check payment was due on a holiday and there was no mail delivery, so the check was not received in time. Or maybe the consumer unwittingly spent more than the credit line. Some consumers set up mechanisms to pay their bills regularly, but were ambushed when payment due dates changed from month to month. In these cases, the consumer would be charged an unexpected fee.

The CARD Act took action to address these problems. The law set standards for when late fees can be assessed. Congress established that credit card bills must be due on the same date each month and that card issuers generally cannot charge a late fee unless consumers are given at least 21 days to pay their bill. The law also established limits on how much can be charged in late fees. As a result, we found that the average size of late fees declined since the passage of the CARD Act. Based on the credit card accounts we studied, representing most of the market, we estimate that the average late fee decreased by $6 after the CARD Act took effect. That means that these consumers paid $1.5 billion less in late fees in 2012 than they would have paid had late fees remained at their pre-CARD Act levels.

The CARD Act also tackled over-limit fees, which often surprised those consumers who had no idea that they had spent past their credit limit. Prior to the law, card issuers could charge a fee for transactions that put cardholders over their credit limit, and each over-limit transaction could result in an additional fee. The CARD Act barred companies from charging a fee to cardholders who exceed their credit limit unless the cardholder has affirmatively opted in to pay over-limit fees. Additionally, card issuers can no longer charge more than one over-limit fee during a billing cycle. With these changes, over-limit fees have been largely eliminated as a source of cost to consumers and revenue to issuers. Based on the credit card accounts that we studied, we estimate that if everything else had remained equal except for the changes made by the CARD Act, those consumers would have paid about $2.5 billion more in over-limit fees in 2012 than they actually paid.

We did find that annual fees and interest rates have increased since 2008, which indicates a shift from hidden back-end pricing toward more transparent front-end pricing that consumers can understand and evaluate more easily. Even more significantly, however, we found that the total cost of credit, which includes all fees and finance charges, declined between 2008 and 2012 by two percentage points.

Consumers were also struggling with a lack of transparency when it came to their credit cards. Credit card agreements were long and difficult to understand. These agreements often contained provisions which allowed the credit card issuer to hike the rate if the consumer tripped any of several complicated wires, including the notorious "universal default." Cardholders would open their monthly statements and be surprised to find that their interest rate had jumped. Credit card agreements also allowed issuers to change the terms at any time and for any reason, and the new terms could be applied to existing balances. Such price changes made it difficult for consumers to predict the cost of their credit card and manage their finances accordingly. The CARD Act sought to make credit card costs clearer to consumers – and we found that it dramatically improved overall transparency in the market.

In order to address unexpected interest rate hikes, the CARD Act generally stopped card issuers from increasing the interest rate on an existing balance unless the cardholder has missed two consecutive payments. The law also added new requirements for monthly statements. Now the statements must include useful information like how long it will take to pay off the bill if the consumer pays only the minimum amount due and how much doing so will cost the consumer. These disclosures give consumers a clearer sense of the consequences in deciding how to handle their credit card payments.

The CARD Act's new disclosure requirements and the end of surprise interest rate increases resulted in a market where pricing is more predictable and transparent for consumers. In this market, shopping for a credit card and comparing costs are far more straightforward. And every credit card user can now make a purchase confident that when the bill comes due, the interest rate will not have skyrocketed without notice. They can count on the fact that if they make their payments on time, the terms of the deal they made at the time of purchase are the terms of the deal they will live with over time.

We also determined that credit card contracts have become shorter and easier to understand in recent years. Our report showed that the card agreements we studied from the largest card issuers have decreased by more than 2,000 words on average and that readability has gone up – making the market more accessible and transparent for consumers. This is not something the CARD Act required, but it is something that we have been urging in order to help consumers process the key information more easily and "know before they owe." Many card issuers have chosen to embrace the spirit of the new law in this respect. We applaud those who are making this effort, we will continue to push others to follow their lead, and we remain willing to work with credit card issuers in finding ways to serve their customers better.

Consumers have responded positively to these market-wide changes. When JD Power released its 2013 U.S. Credit Card Satisfaction Study, it showed credit card satisfaction at an all-time high since the study was first conducted. Significantly, the study concluded that "overall, customers appear to be increasingly happy with their credit cards" and JD Power attributed some of that satisfaction to the CARD Act.

We also believe that the increasing satisfaction customers are expressing about their credit cards reflects the manner in which some issuers have intensified their focus on customer complaints. More operations are prioritizing and incentivizing efforts to remediate individual complaints and to analyze and respond to patterns in the complaints they receive. These are powerful market developments that naturally improve customer service and customer loyalty. They also pay tangible dividends by reducing legal risk, reputational risk, and regulatory risk.

In order to get a complete view of changes in the credit card market, we examined the overall availability of credit. Credit availability started declining in 2008 – before the CARD Act had even passed, but after the financial crisis had begun – and by most measures began to rebound in 2009. This is not surprising, as credit is known to be cyclical and the nation's economy was experiencing its sharpest downturn in decades. So as the crisis hit, credit losses ensued, and creditors implemented more restrictive credit standards. Even with the changes that occurred during those unusual economic conditions, consumers with credit cards still have plenty of available credit overall. In fact, there is currently about $2 trillion worth of unused credit in the market.

The CARD Act has provisions that were explicitly designed to better protect young consumers from getting credit cards they cannot afford. In the years prior to the CARD Act, it was often too easy for students to rack up credit card debt they could not pay back and damage their credit rating for years to come. When I was serving as the Treasurer of Ohio, I heard many bitter complaints from parents about the aggressive marketing practices on college campuses that targeted naïve 18-year-olds just away from home for the first time. With the CARD Act, consumers under the age of 21 cannot get a credit card unless they can demonstrate an independent ability to repay the debt or unless they have a cosigner over the age of 21. Our report found that the number of credit card holders under 21 has been cut in half in recent years. This decrease, which contributes to the decline in available credit, is an intended consequence of the CARD Act and is good news in promoting responsible access to credit.

We have seen two other factors that may be contributing to the dip in available credit. First, we have seen a notable drop in the number of consumers who receive unsolicited credit limit increases on their accounts – meaning that more consumers have to ask for their credit limit to be raised rather than having it happen automatically. Second, the ability-to-repay provisions in the new law have had at least a modest effect on credit availability. We have seen that at least a small slice of consumers whom card issuers may deem to be creditworthy have been declined for credit cards because they cannot prove they have the means to pay back the potential debt. We addressed one such issue that came to our attention by issuing a new regulation earlier this year. This rule made it easier for stay-at-home spouses or partners to get their own card if they have access to resources that allow them to make payments. Consumers need access to credit; we simply want to ensure that they have responsible access to credit.

Although the CARD Act effectively addressed many problematic practices in the market, we do highlight a number of outstanding concerns in our report. One area of concern is credit card add-on products, where we have seen first-hand how the deceptive marketing of these products can harm consumers. The Bureau has already issued a bulletin to put issuers on notice of these problems, and we have brought several enforcement actions that have put more than $700 million back in the pockets of consumers. We will continue to use both our supervisory and enforcement authorities to protect consumers by rooting out unfair, deceptive, or abusive acts or practices.

Second, we recognize that some card issuers charge upfront fees that exceed 25% of the initial credit limit, which is the cap on fees that the CARD

Act sought to impose, but those practices have been held not to be covered by the law because a portion of the fees are paid prior to account opening. We plan to keep a close eye on how card issuers use application fees in connection with opening accounts, and we will determine if we should take action under our available authorities.

Third, we plan to study the impact of deferred interest products. These are credit cards that come with a 0% interest rate but with a catch. If the balance is not paid in full by a certain time, the company will assess interest retroactively. The data we obtained indicates that over 40 percent of borrowers with subprime credit histories end up being charged retroactive interest. We will be examining the risks and benefits of such products and will take action if it appears to be justified.

Fourth, we have identified a number of areas in which transparency concerns remain. One such area relates to online disclosures. While the CARD Act requires certain disclosures to appear on monthly statements, those consumers who pay their bills online may not see the disclosures. We will be monitoring the steps that card issuers take to provide consumers with these beneficial disclosures when they access their accounts in different ways.

Fifth, we are concerned about the quality of disclosures that are made about rewards products. Many consumers are picking their credit cards based on rewards programs. These offers, however, can be highly complex, as consumers may face detailed and confusing rules about how they can actually use their rewards. We will be reviewing whether rewards disclosures are being made in a clear and transparent manner, and we will consider whether additional protections are needed.

Lastly, we are concerned about the disclosures used to inform consumers about grace periods. Most cards allow consumers to avoid paying interest on purchases when they pay their balance in full each month. This period between the end of a billing cycle and the payment due date is called the "grace period." We want to make sure consumers know that once they carry a credit card balance into a new month, they no longer have a grace period on new purchases. While we have not yet studied the level of consumer understanding about grace periods and how they work, it is an area that merits our future attention.

Our CARD Act report was a comprehensive undertaking which showed that, on the whole, the CARD Act accomplished a number of its intended goals. Based on the information we have available to review changes in the credit card market, the Act eliminated many unfair fees, made some market practices more transparent, paved the way for easier comparison shopping, and created a market where consumers can see the costs upfront. These changes are critical to strengthening consumer protections in the marketplace and helping us rebuild our economy.

Today's report was based on extensive research. We looked at data spanning the period from before the law was passed through December 2012. To dispel any myths, let me just say that we use anonymized industry data to better understand how the markets are working. We never receive a card holder's name or other direct or unique identifiers, we never receive information describing the specific transactions on any account, and we do not monitor any individual's financial transactions. We are only interested in market trends, and as a result, the data is limited to items like interest rates, account balances, total purchases, total payments, and fees charged to consumers. In fact, for purposes of this report, industry participants submitted to us analyses they developed from similar data. Without all of this information, we would not be able to study the market, to understand the benefits of the CARD Act, and to flag areas of possible risks to consumers. In short, we would not be effective in carrying out our responsibility to report to Congress and the American public.

Today, I am looking forward to vigorous discussions about the state of the credit card market and the impact of the CARD Act on both consumers and the industry. Thank you for joining us.

In: Credit Card Accountability Responsibility … ISBN: 978-1-62948-689-5
Editor: Oliver P. Meyer

Chapter 2

CARD ACT REPORT: A REVIEW OF THE IMPACT OF THE CARD ACT ON THE CONSUMER CREDIT MARKET*

Consumer Financial Protection Bureau

EXECUTIVE SUMMARY

The Credit Card Accountability Responsibility and Disclosure Act of 2009 ("CARD Act" or "the Act") changed the landscape of the credit card market. The CARD Act was enacted to "establish fair and transparent practices related to the extension of credit" in this market, regulating both the underwriting and pricing of credit card accounts.[1] Among other things, the Act prohibits credit card issuers from extending credit without assessing the consumer's ability to pay, with special rules regarding the extension of credit to persons under the age of 21. The Act restricts the amount of "upfront" fees that an issuer can charge during the first year after an account is opened, and limits the instances in which issuers can charge "back-end" penalty fees when a consumer makes a late payment or exceeds his or her credit limit. The Act also restricts the circumstances under which issuers can increase interest rates on credit cards and establishes procedures for doing so.

---

* This is an edited, reformatted and augmented version of the Consumer Financial Protection Bureau, dated October 1, 2013.

Implementation of the CARD Act was vested originally with the Board of Governors of the Federal Reserve System ("Board"), and passed to the Consumer Financial Protection Bureau ("CFPB" or "Bureau") on July 21, 2011, pursuant to the Dodd-Frank Wall Street Reform and Consumer Protection Act ("Dodd-Frank Act"). The CARD Act directs the Bureau to conduct a biennial review of the consumer credit card market, including the effect of the Act on the cost and availability of credit and the adequacy of protections for consumers relating to credit card plans. This is the first such report the Bureau has prepared. The report draws upon publicly and commercially available data as well as data obtained by the Bureau through its supervision of large credit card issuers.*

Based on our analysis of the data, as well as our experience monitoring the credit card market for risks to consumers, we present the following findings.

Cost of Credit

The CARD Act has impacted the way that consumers pay for credit in the credit card marketplace and has significantly enhanced transparency for consumers. Overlimit fees and repricing actions have been largely eliminated; those effects can be directly traced to the Act. The dollar amount of late fees is down as well, and the CARD Act directly caused this reduction.

The end result is a market in which shopping for a credit card and comparing costs is far more straightforward than it was prior to enactment of the Act. Many credit card agreements have become shorter and easier to understand, though it is not clear how much of these changes can be attributed directly to the CARD Act since it did not explicitly mandate changes to the length and form of credit card agreements. Limitations on "back-end" fees, along with restrictions on an issuer's ability to raise interest rates, have simplified a consumer's cost calculations. Credit card costs are now more closely related to the clearly disclosed annual fees and interest rates. This greater transparency means a consumer deciding whether to charge a purchase can now make that decision with far more confidence that costs will be a function of the current interest rate rather than some yet-to-be determined interest rate that could be reassessed at any time and for any reason by the issuer.

* The CFPB considers all supervisory information to be confidential. Consistent with the Bureau's rules, the data findings presented in this paper do not directly or indirectly identify the institutions or consumers involved. *See* 12 C.F.R. § 1070.41(c).

Consistent with the shift towards more transparency as a result of upfront pricing, we find that, beginning in early 2009 and continuing through February 2010, when many provisions of the Act went into effect, the interest rate on credit card accounts increased, while back-end fees decreased or were eliminated. While some of this increase was likely intended to offset other changes in pricing affected by the CARD Act, we make no judgment on the extent to which the CARD Act, as distinguished from other factors such as the impact of the Great Recession, contributed to these increases.

However, we do find that among the card issuers represented in the Bureau's credit card database (representing between 85% and 90% of credit card industry balances), the total cost of credit – i.e. the annualized sum of all amounts paid by consumers (including both interest charges and fees) divided by the average of outstanding balances – *declined* by 194 basis points from Q4 2008 to Q4 2012. Again, it is unclear how much of that change is attributable to the CARD Act.

Availability of Credit

Differentiating between the willingness of creditors to extend credit and the desire of consumers to avail themselves of that credit is challenging. To better understand credit availability, we consider a number of measures, including the volume of credit card mail solicitations, the volume of new account originations, the approval rates on credit card applications, the size of credit lines granted to new accounts, and the frequency with which credit lines are increased.

From these metrics, a clear pattern emerges: beginning in 2008, prior to the enactment of the CARD Act, but after the onset of the Great Recession, credit became less available in the credit card marketplace. Credit availability bottomed out in 2009 and has since risen, although not to 2007 levels. The decline was smaller and the subsequent increase more robust among consumers with stronger credit scores than among those with subprime credit scores.

This pattern is consistent with trends observed in other consumer credit markets during the same time frame. The post-2009 recovery in the credit card market has been more robust than that of some markets (such as home equity lines of credit), while lagging behind that of others (such as auto lending).

According to the Bureau's data, total credit line (whether used or unused) was $200 billion lower at the end of 2012 than when many provisions of the

CARD Act took effect in February 2010. This decline disproportionately occurred in the subprime credit space. The industry contraction that we observe began before the enactment of the CARD Act and has continued through 2012, though at a slower pace than during the peak of the Great Recession. Even so, consumers still possessed $1.9 trillion in unused credit line at the end of 2012.

The evidence suggests that the CARD Act had a discernible impact on credit availability in three discrete respects. First, there has been a substantial decrease in the number of credit card accounts originated among students and other consumers under the age of 21. Second, the issuers contacted in preparing this report stated that a small but discernible percentage of applicants that they deemed otherwise creditworthy are being declined as a result of insufficient income to satisfy the Act's ability-to-pay requirement. Third, and relatedly, there has been a marked decline in the percentage of consumers receiving unsolicited credit line increases (also referred to as "proactive line increases") on their accounts. At least some of these limitations on access to credit appear to be intended consequences of the CARD Act's stated objective of creating fair and transparent practices with respect to open-end credit.

Remaining Concerns

The CARD Act made sweeping changes in the credit card marketplace and addressed many of the practices that consumer advocates and others had identified as particularly problematic.[2] Voluntary actions by card issuers, including renewed attention to customer service and complaints, have brought about further market improvements. Additionally, the Bureau is continuing its work with card issuers on voluntary efforts to shorten and simplify cardholder agreements.

There remain, however, some possible areas of concern – practices that may pose risks to consumers and may warrant further scrutiny by the Bureau. Based on the work that supports this report and our other activities, we identify six examples of such practices:

1. **Add-on Products:** Credit card issuers market various "add-on" products to card users, including debt protection, identity theft protection, credit score monitoring, and other products that are supplementary to the actual extension of credit. The Bureau has found

through its supervisory work that these products are frequently sold in a manner that harms consumers. The Bureau has engaged in enforcement actions and issued a bulletin[3] that provides industry guidance on the marketing of these products. The Bureau will continue to closely review the sale of add-on products by card issuers and their service providers to determine whether additional actions are warranted.

2. **Fee Harvester Cards:** Some card issuers charge upfront fees that exceed 25% of a card's initial credit limit, but those practices have been held not to be covered by the CARD Act because a portion of the fees are paid prior to account opening. The Bureau will continue to monitor the use of application fees in connection with account opening to determine if it should take action under its available authorities.
3. **Deferred Interest Products:** In the private label credit card market, it is common to offer promotional financing for purchases. These offers retroactively assess and charge interest if the balance is not paid in full by a specific date. The evidence gathered by the Bureau indicates that for borrowers with subprime credit scores, about 43% are ultimately charged retroactive interest in a lump sum. The Bureau intends to continue to study these issues and assess whether additional action is appropriate to promote a more fair and transparent market.
4. **Transparency Issues**
    a. **Online Disclosures:** The CARD Act mandated that certain disclosures be included on monthly billing statements, including warnings related to late fees and the cost to the consumer of making only the minimum payment due. Regulation Z adds other requirements for these statements. However, consumers who pay their bills electronically may not access their monthly statement and instead may use online portals which are not required to contain these disclosures. This reflects a more general challenge of translating regulations related to disclosures largely written for a paper-and-pencil world into the modern electronic world. The Bureau will observe closely how card issuers ensure that consumers receive disclosures in different channels.
    b. **Rewards Products:** For certain consumers, comparison shopping for new credit cards frequently revolves around considering different rewards programs. Rewards offers can be highly complex, with detailed rules regarding the eligibility for sign-on

bonuses, the value of earned points, the rate at which they are earned, and the rules governing their forfeiture. In the course of its consumer research and market monitoring activities, the Bureau will review whether rewards disclosures are being made in a clear and transparent manner, as well as assess whether additional action is warranted.

c. **Grace Periods:** For consumers who do not pay their balance in full each month, a key determinant of their cost of credit is the grace period. It is unclear whether consumers understand that once they carry a balance into a new month, interest will be assessed on the unpaid balance from the start of the prior month. Until the consumer qualifies for the grace period again, interest is assessed on all purchases from the date of purchase. It is likewise unclear whether consumers understand that even after they pay the full amount shown on their bill, they may still owe "trailing interest" for the period from the time the bill was issued until the time the payment was received. As with rewards products, the Bureau will review whether grace period limitations are being disclosed in a clear and transparent manner.

1. INTRODUCTION

Implementation of the Credit Card Accountability Responsibility and Disclosure Act of 2009 ("CARD Act") was vested originally with the Board of Governors of the Federal Reserve System ("Board"),[4] and passed to the Consumer Financial Protection Bureau ("CFPB" or "Bureau") on July 21, 2011, pursuant to the Dodd-Frank Wall Street Reform and Consumer Protection Act ("Dodd-Frank Act").[5] Section 502(a) of the CARD Act requires periodic reviews of the consumer credit card market, within the limits of the Bureau's existing resources available for reporting purposes.[*] This review is required every two years beginning two years after the effective date of the CARD Act,[6] or alternatively, two years after a material revision of the regulations on consumer credit card plans.[7] In April 2011, the Board made

[*] As enacted in 2009, the CARD Act directed that the Board conduct this review. *See* 15 U.S.C. § 1616(a) (2012). The Bureau and the Board concluded in May 2012 that responsibility for this review transferred to the CFPB, along with the general transfer of rulemaking authority for the Truth in Lending Act.

material changes to the rules it issued to implement the CARD Act.[8] Those revisions became effective on October 1, 2011, making this October 2013 report the first iteration of this biennial requirement.

As set forth in the statute, this review seeks to examine developments in the consumer credit card marketplace, including:

1. Terms of credit card agreements and the practices of credit card issuers;
2. Effectiveness of disclosure of terms, fees, and other expenses of credit card plans;
3. Adequacy of protections against unfair or deceptive acts or practices relating to credit card plans; and
4. Whether or not, and to what extent, the implementation of this Act and the amendments made by this Act has affected:
   a. cost and availability of credit, particularly with respect to non-prime borrowers;
   b. the safety and soundness of credit card issuers;[c*]
   c. the use of risk-based pricing; or
   d. credit card product innovation.

1.1. Overview of the CARD Act

Since 1968, the Truth in Lending Act ("TILA") has been the principal federal law regulating the credit card marketplace.[9] Prior to passage of the CARD Act, which amended TILA, the provisions of TILA and its implementing regulation ("Regulation Z")[10] that applied to open-end unsecured credit focused principally on disclosure requirements related to product pricing terms and periodic statements, but otherwise placed few substantive limits on industry pricing practices.

In addition to TILA, credit card issuers also have been subject to the provisions of Section 5 of the Federal Trade Commission Act which prohibits "unfair or deceptive acts or practices." In December 2008, the Board, along with the National Credit Union Administration ("NCUA") and Office of Thrift Supervision ("OTS"), promulgated amendments to their regulations on unfair

[*] This report does not address specific safety and soundness issues relating to credit card issuers. The prudential regulators have the primary responsibility for monitoring the safety and soundness of financial institutions. The Bureau therefore does not have detailed data on specific safety and soundness issues.

or deceptive acts or practices ("UDAP rules") which substantively regulated certain credit card practices.[11] Those amendments were scheduled to take effect on August 1, 2010.

The CARD Act was signed into law in May 2009. Passage of the Act was expressly intended to "establish fair and transparent practices related to the extension of credit" in the credit card market.[12] To achieve these objectives, the Act added into TILA a number of new substantive protections for consumers, expanding upon some of the provisions that had been included in the UDAP rules and addressing other issues as well. Included in Appendix A is a timeline of events and activities surrounding the CARD Act.

The Board implemented the CARD Act through amendments to Regulation Z,[13] and the Bureau subsequently reissued these rules in December 2011.[14] The following is a high-level summary of principal changes contained in the CARD Act and the implementing regulations.

Interest Rate Increases[15]

The Act limits the circumstances under which credit card issuers can increase interest rates on existing balances and the circumstances under which issuers can change the interest rate applicable to future transactions. For changes affecting only future transactions, the card issuer generally must give the consumer 45 days written notice of a rate increase. Furthermore, during the first year after an account is opened, issuers generally are prohibited from increasing the interest rate except in limited circumstances, such as the expiration of promotional rates or a change in the variable rate to which the credit card interest rate is linked. For interest rate increases applicable to existing balances, the card issuer generally cannot increase the rate unless the consumer has missed two consecutive monthly payments (i.e. 60 days past due) and the consumer has been provided 45 days written notice.

In addition, after an issuer increases the interest rate on an account – either for existing balances or for new transactions – the issuer is generally required to review the account at least once every six months to determine whether the factors underlying the increase have changed and to reduce the interest rate where indicated by the review.

Penalty Fee Restrictions[16]

Penalty fees, such as late fees or overlimit fees, must now be "reasonable and proportional" to the relevant violation of account terms. The implementing rules establish a safe harbor for reasonable and proportional late fees of $25[17] for a first late payment and $35 for each subsequent violation within the next six months.

Overlimit Fee Opt-in[18]

There are additional restrictions on the overlimit fees assessed when a consumer exceeds his or her assigned credit line. Per the Act, issuers may only charge such fees if the consumer expressly opts in to permit overlimit transactions.

Fee Harvester Cards[19]

The CARD Act and implementing regulations provide that an issuer may not require consumers to pay fees (other than penalty fees) during the first year in which an account is opened which exceed 25% of the total initial credit line.[20]

Payment Timing[21]

Payments must now be due on the same day of each month. In addition, the Act and implementing regulations contain a set of rules as to which payments must be considered timely. There are also rules requiring issuers to adopt reasonable procedures designed to assure that periodic statements are mailed or delivered at least 21 days before the payment is due.

Payment Allocation[22]

Subject to certain exceptions, when a consumer makes a payment on his or her account, issuers are now required to allocate the amount of that payment that exceeds the minimum payment first to balances that are subject to highest interest rates and then to each successive balance bearing the next highest rate of interest.

Monthly Statements[23]

Monthly statements must describe how long it would take the consumer—and how much it would cost—to pay the full balance on the card by paying only the required minimum monthly payment. For comparison, the statement must also show the monthly payment required to repay the full balance in three years if no further transactions are made, and the total cost to the consumer if the balance is paid in three years. Monthly statements must also contain a conspicuous warning of the amount of the late fee and any penalty rate that may be imposed if the minimum payment is not received by the due date.

Ability to Pay[24]

Card issuers cannot open a credit card account or increase a credit line on a card account unless the card issuer considers the ability of the consumer to make the required payments under the terms of the account. The implementing regulations state that such consideration should include the ratio of debt obligations to income, the ratio of debt obligations to assets, or the income available to the consumer after paying debt obligations. The regulations permit the use of a predictive model to estimate income as long as the model is statistically sound.

In May 2013, the Bureau amended the rules implementing the credit card ability-to-pay provisions of TILA to address concerns that the rules unduly limited the ability of spouses and partners not working outside the home to obtain credit cards based on the income of their spouse or partner. The final rule removed the requirement that issuers consider consumers' independent ability to pay for applicants who are 21 or older. Instead, issuers may now consider income and assets to which such consumers have a reasonable expectation of access.

Students and Younger Cardholders[25]

The Act imposed new restrictions related to on-campus or near-campus marketing of credit cards. In addition, any credit card applicant under 21 years of age must demonstrate his or her independent ability to make payments on the account or have a co-signer that is 21 or older with the ability to make payments. Card issuers also are prohibited from sending pre-approved offers of credit to persons under age 21 unless the individual consents to receiving such offers.

1.2. Methodology, Data Sources, and Limitations

In light of the complexity of undertaking this review, the Bureau sought to leverage as many data sources as were reasonably available. Such sources include:

1. De-identified loan-level information from a sample of large banks' credit card portfolios, which is compiled in the CFPB's Credit Card Database ("CCDB"). The data is updated monthly and covers the period from January 2008 to December 2012. The database contains information on the full consumer and small business credit card

portfolios, representing between 85% and 90% of credit card industry balances. Information in the database cannot be tied to any particular individual nor can multiple accounts in the database that may belong to a single individual be linked in any way. The database does include anonymous updating of accounts over time in order to discern changes in account information such as annual percentage rates ("APR"), balances, payments, interest charges, and fees;[*]

2. Responses to a Credit Card Practices Inquiry ("CCPI") conducted by the CFPB Office of Supervision gathering information from a number of large banks on their credit card and CARD Act compliance practices. The issuers that participated in this inquiry represent approximately 80% of credit card industry balances;
3. Responses to a Request for Information ("RFI") published in the Federal Register in December 2012 wherein the Bureau sought comment on the terms of credit card agreements and practices of credit card issuers, the effectiveness of credit card disclosure, the adequacy of protection from unfair or deceptive acts or practices, whether the CARD Act affected the cost and availability of credit, whether the CARD Act has impacted issuer safety and soundness, whether the CARD Act had any effect on the use of risk-based pricing, and whether the CARD Act had any impact on credit card innovation.[26] The RFI generated 31 responses, including responses from 3 trade associations representing credit card issuers, 6 individual issuers, and 4 consumer advocacy groups;[27]
4. Data from the CFPB Consumer Credit Panel, which contains de-identified credit reports for a representative sample of the US population, refreshed on a quarterly basis;
5. Commercially available data sources that focus on the credit card industry, including mail volume monitoring reports, industry analyst reports, and data services and analytics from industry consultants. As an example, Experian and Oliver Wyman collaborate to produce the quarterly "Market Intelligence Report," which covers product trends

[*] The Bureau recognizes that the issuers who supply data to the CCDB constitute a non-random sample in that they are the largest issuers. The practices and experiences of these issuers are not necessarily representative of the practices and experiences of many small credit card issuers. Thus, we do not attempt in this report to extrapolate from the CCDB data to make projections for the entire market. However, because the participating issuers represent 85%-90% of credit card industry balances, the Bureau is confident that the findings reported here would not materially change if data from the entire universe of card issuers were available.

in consumer finance, including those in credit card, mortgage, and auto lending markets; and

6. Numerous public sources such as:
   a. SEC filings, analyst presentations, reports and studies prepared by other government agencies, and congressional testimony and hearings on the CARD Act;
   b. Materials presented at the CFPB's 2011 CARD Act Conference where industry executives, leading academics, and consumer advocates examined the effects of the CARD Act; and
   c. The Federal Reserve Bank of New York's published reports on findings derived from a random sample of consumer credit reports.

FICO Score Ranges

This review frequently focuses on trends within specific subsets of the credit spectrum. The population of accountholders in the CCDB is analyzed based on risk scoring models developed by the Fair Isaac Corporation ("FICO"). The FICO scores submitted by credit card issuers to the CCDB are based on the scoring model in use by that institution at a given point in time.[28] Accounts are split into four FICO score ranges, shown in the table below with approximate proportions of the scored population of the United States:[29]

FICO Score Ranges	% of US Population with a Credit Score
Superprime (FICO scores ≥ 720)	45%
Prime (FICO scores 660-719)	20%
Core Subprime (FICO scores 620-659)	10%
Deep Subprime (FICO scores < 620)	25%t

FICO scores in the CCDB are refreshed regularly. Refreshed scores are used throughout this report to place accounts into score ranges for the analyses presented here, with the exception of analyses performed on account-origination data, which use the FICO score at origination. As a result, when analyzing trends over time within a particular FICO score range, we are not analyzing a constant set of accounts, but rather accounts that fall within that range at each point in time under analysis.

Untangling Correlation, Causality, and the Great Recession

One of the most reliable methods of assessing causality is to track and compare the performance of otherwise identically-situated individuals, some of whom are subject to a particular intervention and others of whom are not. Needless to say, there is no control group of US consumer credit card accounts or issuers that were not subject to the CARD Act, and thus this review is limited in what can be causally attributed to the CARD Act.

Additionally, gauging the impact of the CARD Act is especially difficult in light of the financial crisis that coincided with the Act's passage. The Act was passed in May of 2009, falling in the midst of the Great Recession as designated by the National Bureau of Economic Research (December 2007 – June 2009).[30] During this crisis, the number of unemployed individuals more than doubled from 2008 to 2009, rising from 7 million to 15 million.[31] The resulting distress contributed to a substantial increase in credit card charge-offs, which increased from 5.1% to 10.8% during this time frame.[32] In reaction to these macroeconomic trends and rapidly increasing charge-offs, and in an attempt to protect against further deterioration in credit performance, credit card issuers sought to reduce their exposure by closing accounts, decreasing unused credit lines, and tightening the criteria for granting new credit or for increasing lines on existing accounts. In addition, the increase in loan losses may have led to increases in pricing to mitigate the impact of the charge-offs. As a result, where we observe substantial changes in issuer and consumer behavior, the question remains whether such changes constituted a response to the CARD Act or a response to the significant financial upheaval taking place during the same time frame.

In addition, any analysis of CARD Act effects is further complicated by the Board, NCUA and OTS adoption of UDAP rules in December 2008 with effective dates beginning in 2010. While some of these rules were ultimately superseded by the Act and its associated rulemakings, the proposal that the agencies issued in May 2008 nevertheless provided significant advance warning to issuers about the likely future direction regulation would take with the enactment of the CARD Act. This may have impacted issuer behavior prior to the Act's passage.

Lastly, although the Act was passed in May 2009, many of its provisions, including restrictions on the repricing of existing balances, did not take effect until February 2010.[33] During this nine- month period, issuers may have made preemptive modifications in advance of the Act even though it had yet to become legally binding.

To address these concerns, this review employs a variety of analytical approaches using the data sources described above. For example, the primary data source for much of this report is the CCDB, which begins in 2008, and as a result our analysis generally starts in 2008 as well. Nonetheless, where availability and reliability permit, this review considers information dating back to as early as 2007. To be clear, the prevailing economic climate in 2007 was appreciably different from conditions following the Act's passage, so these comparisons are necessarily imperfect. We believe this approach succeeds in generating insights relating to the credit card marketplace, and provides at least a directional indication of the impact of the CARD Act, though not the precise magnitude.

Where appropriate, this review also looks beyond the immediate consumer credit card space to draw relevant parallels to trends observed across the consumer financial marketplace, including for such products as mortgages and auto loans. In addition, in a number of places throughout this review, we compare the consumer credit card market with the small business credit card market. While both are unsecured open-end credit products with similar structures, the CARD Act applies only to consumer credit cards and not to small business credit cards. As such, any similarities in trends in the cost and availability of credit between these two markets post-CARD Act may suggest that such trends are likely attributable to something affecting both card types, such as a macroeconomic event like the Great Recession. Conversely, where consumer cards and small business cards show dissimilarities, one could plausibly point to the CARD Act as a potential contributing factor. In some cases, issuers enacted CARD Act changes in their small business portfolios and, where we are aware of such actions, we excluded these portfolios from the comparison analysis for both consumer and small business cards. The comparison only includes issuers that participate in both the consumer card and small business card markets in order to reduce the impact of issuer-dependent differences in strategy on our analyses.

2. Cost of Credit

2.1. Definition

One question that Congress directed the Bureau to study is "whether and to what extent the implementation of the Act has affected the cost of credit, particularly with respect to non-prime borrowers."[34] In approaching this question, it is important to recognize that the cost of credit has many components.

Consumers who utilize a credit card may pay for that credit in a number of different ways. Consumers may be charged an annual (or monthly) fee. They may incur penalty fees if they violate the account terms, most commonly by making a late payment or a transaction that exceeds his or her credit limit. They may be charged a variety of other fees such as cash advance fees, balance transfer fees, or foreign transaction fees. Finally, consumers may pay interest charges. In general, these interest charges are only paid when a consumer carries over a balance from month to month, although for certain types of balances (such as cash advances) interest charges may be assessed from the date of the transaction so that a consumer who pays the entire balance on time still incurs an interest charge.

The CARD Act directly regulated practices with respect to penalty fees and interest rate increases triggered by delinquent or otherwise "risky" behavior. We therefore begin by evaluating the impact of the CARD Act on those components of pricing. We then examine trends in other components of pricing, including annual and other fees and interest rates and interest charges.[*]

A change in the cost of a component of pricing can have a significant impact on a market, even if the overall effect is neutral from a cost perspective, because the components may not all be equally salient to or predictable for consumers when making purchasing and borrowing decisions. For example, consumers may focus on a credit card's advertised interest rate and compare products along this dimension, rather than compare products across multiple other dimensions, such as penalty interest rates or penalty fees. Thus, to the extent that regulation shifts costs either towards or away from salient components, it can significantly affect consumers in the market.[†]

Although changes in component costs and the composition of pricing are therefore important to consider, the ultimate question posed to the Bureau

[*] The CARD Act and implementing regulations also provide that issuers may not require consumers to pay fees (except penalty fees) during the first year after account opening that exceed 25% of the consumer's credit limit. The issuers represented in the CCDB did not charge fees at the level regulated by the Act and thus we cannot observe the impact of this change through the data available to us.

[†] For example, Oren Bar-Gill and Ryan Bubb assert that high back-end fees were used by credit card issuers because these fees are not salient to consumers. As part of their analysis, the authors cite behavioral economics work showing that customers "place excessive weight on short-term, salient prices and insufficient weight on long-term, non-salient prices." Oren Bar-Gill & Ryan Bubb, *Credit Card Pricing: The CARD Act and Beyond*, 97 Cornell L. Rev. 967, 969 (2012).

concerns the "cost of credit." To measure all-in costs, we calculate, on a monthly basis, a metric that includes everything that consumers pay to possess and use their credit cards and state that total as a percentage of the average cycle- ending balance on an annualized basis for those accounts. This "Total Cost of Credit" ("TCC") metric incorporates all fees and interest charges the consumer pays to the issuer. It excludes revenue generated though separate agreements between other businesses and the issuer, such as interchange fees paid by merchants and marketing fees or commissions paid by companies offering add-on products to an issuer's customer base. This TCC metric thus captures all of the component costs that consumers pay.*

2.2. Changes in Components of Cost

2.2.1. Overlimit Fees

The CARD Act has had its most direct and immediate effect with respect to the assessment of overlimit fees.

Generally speaking, when a consumer seeks to make a transaction using a credit card, the issuer will receive an instantaneous electronic message seeking authorization for the transaction. Prior to the enactment of the CARD Act, it was a common practice for issuers to authorize transactions which would result in a balance that exceeded the credit limit on the account. Issuers would then assess an overlimit fee either when the transaction settled or at the end of the billing cycle if the account was overlimit at that time.

Beginning in the mid-1990s through 2005, the fees charged for overlimit transactions more than doubled, increasing from under $15 to over $30.[35] By 2008, for the issuers represented in the CCDB, the average overlimit charge was $34.80.

The CARD Act made two changes with respect to overlimit fees. First, the Act prohibits the assessment of such fees unless consumers opt in to such charges.[36] Such opt-ins are revocable at any time by the consumer, and the consumer must be notified of the right to revoke any time an overlimit fee is assessed.[37] Second, the Act requires that overlimit fees, when assessed, be

* Our methodology follows one used by Argus Information & Advisory Services in a presentation it made in collaboration with nine large card issuers at a conference sponsored by the Bureau in 2011. Argus calculated what it termed "gross effective asset yield" which was computed as the sum of interest charges, fees and gross interchange as a percentage of average daily balance. Our calculation of TCC differs from this methodology only by excluding interchange revenue, which is not a cost paid directly by the consumer to the card issuer.

reasonable and proportional to the violation.[38] The implementing rule establishes a "safe harbor" benchmark for "reasonable and proportional" penalty fees: $25 for a first violation and $35 for each subsequent violation within the next six months.[39]

In the wake of these changes, most credit card issuers simply stopped charging overlimit fees altogether. The figure below illustrates this trend, showing overlimit fees declining sharply coincident with the effective date of the CARD Act opt-in rule in February 2010. Even after this elimination of overlimit fees, customers are still being authorized for charges over their credit limit, though less frequently. In Q4 2008, 16.4% of active accounts had one or more overlimit instances, and 48.6% of the time these overlimit occurrences resulted in the assessment of an overlimit fee. This translates into a 7.9% overlimit fee incidence rate in Q4 2008. By comparison, by Q4 2012, 12.7% of active accounts had one or more overlimit instances, but these instances led to the assessment of an overlimit fee only 3.4% of the time. This translates into an overlimit incidence rate of 0.4%.

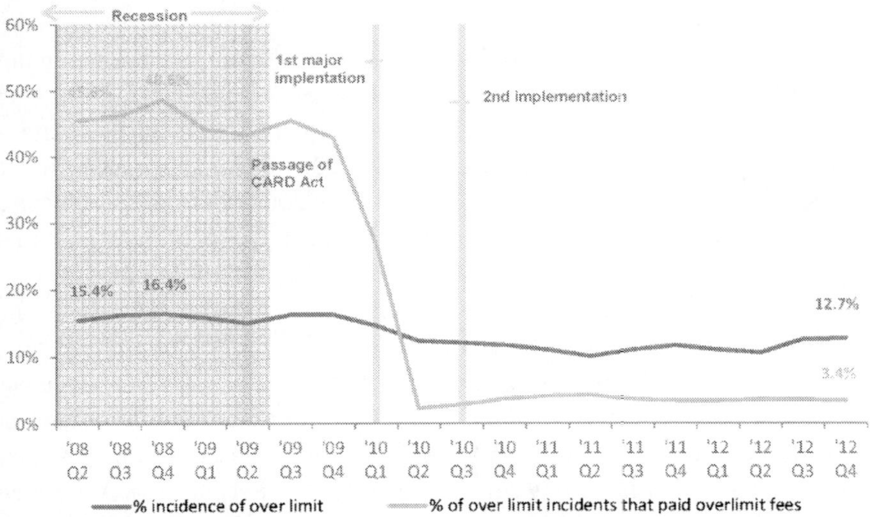

Source: Credit Card Database* number of observations of over limit accounts divided by number of active accounts, and number of accounts paying overlimit fees divided by number of over limit instances

Figure 1. Trends in Overlimit Fees (Active Accounts).

* In the CCDB, accounts are flagged as "active" if the account has had any activity (i.e. any charge or any payment) during the preceding twelve months. We use this definition of active in this report.

It is clear that the CARD Act has effectively eliminated overlimit fees as a source of cost to consumers and revenue to issuers. Had the incidence of overlimit fees remained at 2007 levels 0f 6.4% and had average overlimit fees remained at their 2008 levels, consumers whose accounts are included in the CCDB would have paid an estimated $2.5 billion more in overlimit fees in 2012 than they actually paid.*

It is important to note that the estimated $2.5 billion difference may over- or understate the impact of to the CARD Act. We cannot address the counter-factual question of whether, and if so to what extent, the incidence of overlimit fees would have declined independent of the CARD Act because of changes in consumer behavior (i.e. fewer consumers seeking to make purchases that exceed their credit limit) or because of changes in issuer behavior (i.e. fewer issuers authorizing overlimit transactions). Conversely, the $2.5 billion difference may understate the impact of the CARD Act if, absent the Act, overlimit incidence would have increased from the 2007 baseline or if issuers would have increased the amount they charged per overlimit incident.

2.2.2. Late Fees

For most credit card accounts, if the consumer fails to make the minimum payment by the due date, the consumer will be assessed a late fee. As with overlimit fees, the level of late fees increased rapidly beginning in the mid-1990s, rising from under $15 to over $30 by 2005.[40] For the issuers in the CCDB, late fees rose to an average of $33.08 by 2008. Consumer advocates complained that some issuers were engaging in a range of practices that artificially increased the frequency of late fees.[41]

The CARD Act made a number of changes relating to late fees. First, the Act restricted the circumstances in which a payment may be considered late, such as prohibiting issuers from considering a payment as late if the payment due date was on a date on which the issuer does not receive or accept payments by mail (e.g. weekend or holiday) and the payment was received by mail on the next business day after the due date.[42] Second, the Act added requirements that the payment due date be the same day each month, that billing statements be mailed at least 21 days before that due date, and that statements include a warning of the amount of the late fee and any penalty rate that will be assessed if a payment is late.[43] Third, the Act added a requirement

* This calculation is based on data from Argus Information & Advisory Services, which reported overlimit fee incidence rates for large issuers for the first and third quarters of 2007. Based upon that data, the Bureau calculated a benchmark quarterly overlimit fee incidence rate of 6.4%.

that late fees be reasonable and proportional to the violation.[44] As noted, the implementing rule establishes a "safe harbor" for "reasonable and proportional" penalty fees, set at $25 for a first violation and $35 for each subsequent violation within the next six months.[45]

As the figure below shows, the average late fee declined with the effective date of the safe harbors in the implementing rules, dropping from $33.08 to $23.13.* The average late fee has increased by $3.71, reaching $26.84 in the fourth quarter of 2012; this likely reflects the impact of the safe harbor permitting a $35 late fee if a consumer is late more than once during a six-month period.

Based on the current incidence of late fees in the CCDB, the Bureau estimates that the $6 decrease in the average late fee has resulted in a $1.5 billion reduction in late fees paid by consumers whose accounts are included in the CCDB.

However, to focus solely on the level of late fees may miss any potential effect that the CARD Act may have had on the incidence of late fees. Using the CCDB, we can track the incidence of late fees since 2008, although as noted earlier, using 2008 as the baseline may set up a comparison from an already elevated level (i.e. late fees may have increased by early 2008 as a result of the Great Recession). From the second quarter of 2008 through the fourth quarter of 2009, the incidence of late fees ranged from a high of 26.1% (in Q3 2008) to a low of 24.2% (in Q4 2009). The incidence rate is calculated by taking the number of late fees assessed in the quarter, and dividing that quantity by the average number of active accounts in the quarter. By the second quarter of 2010, the first full quarter after the CARD Act rules governing the assessment of late fees took effect, the late fee incidence rate dropped to 20.0%. The incidence remained relatively constant until the second half of 2012, when the incidence rate increased to 22.2%, where it has held for the past year.

* Most of the late fee provisions in the Card Act were implemented by rules that became effective in February 2010. However, the provisions that require late fees amounts to be reasonable and proportional and establish the safe harbor amounts set forth in the implementing regulations were not effective until August 2010.

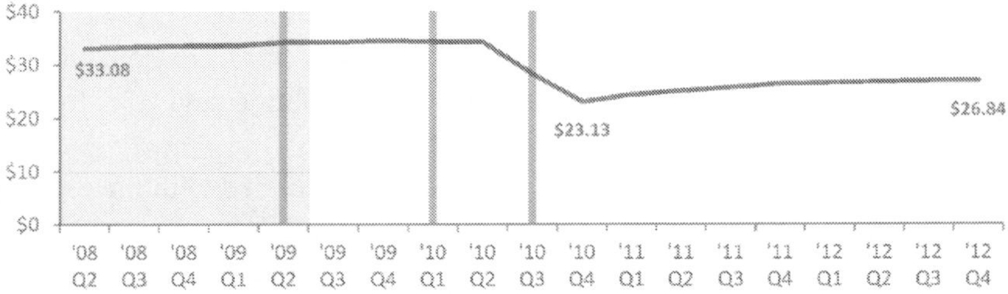

Source: CCDB; Total late fees assessed divided by number of late fees paid.

Figure 2. Average Late Fee.

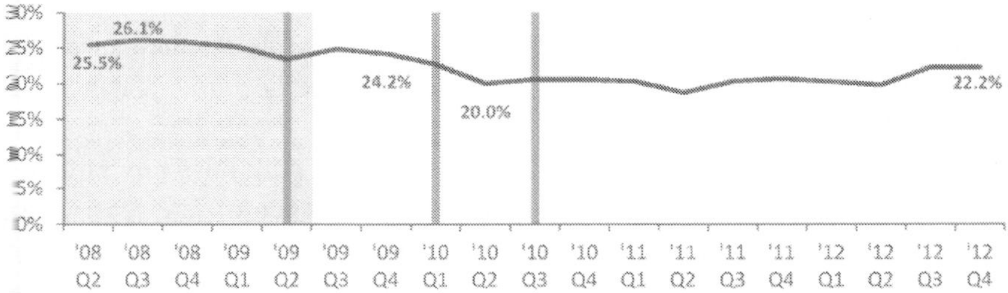

Source: CCDB; number of late fees assessed divided by average number of active accounts.

Figure 3. Quarterly Incidence Rate of Late Fees (Active Accounts).

There are a number of factors independent of the CARD Act that may have contributed to changes in late fee incidence. The Argus data indicate that, in 2007, the late fee incidence rate among nine large issuers was 21.3%; as such, the drop that occurred after most of the late fee provisions in the CARD Act took effect in February 2010 could reflect improvement in the overall economy. Furthermore, there has been an overall shift in the composition of credit card accounts in the CCDB, with accounts with subprime credit scores representing a smaller share of the total today than in 2008. Because accounts with subprime credit scores are more likely to incur penalty fees, it is possible that the decrease in late fee incidence is driven by the decreased proportion of accounts with subprime credit scores in the data.

2.2.3. Annual Fees

The decline in late and overlimit fees was offset to some extent by an increase in the size and frequency of annual fees. As the chart below shows, from Q2 2008 through Q1 2010 the percentage of accounts on which annual fees were charged remained fairly constant.

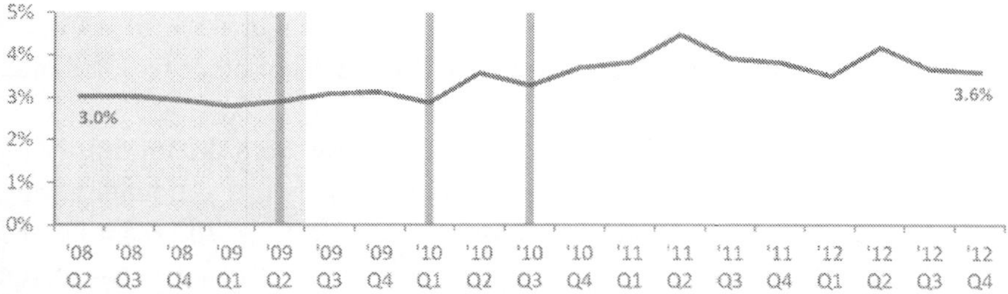

Source: CCDB; number of annual fees assessed divided by number of open accounts.

Figure 4. Quarterly Incidence Rate of Annual Fees (Open Accounts).

Beginning in Q2 2010, coincident with one of the major implementation dates of the CARD Act, there was an increase in the percentage of accounts with annual fees. The percentage increases were largest for accounts with deep subprime credit scores and increased more modestly, although still significantly, for the core subprime and prime segments. This increase in the percentage of accounts with annual fees partially offset the reduction in incidence and amount of late and overlimit fees discussed above.

The average dollar amount of annual fees increased from $32.48 in 2008 to $34.19 in 2012. Using a baseline incidence rate of 3.0% from 2008 through Q1 2010 compared to the 3.75% rate in the year 2012, the Bureau can estimate the increase in annual fees. Due to the increase in both the incidence and average dollar amount of annual fees, consumers with accounts in the CCDB paid an additional $475 million in annual fees in 2012.

In contrast to back-end fees such as overlimit and late fees, the incurrence of an annual fee is certain, making it easier for consumers to anticipate costs. As such, we view the increase in annual fees following the implementation of the CARD Act as part of a shift away from complex and often confusing pricing to pricing that is more predictable and transparent for consumers.

2.2.4. Other Fees

Beyond the fees already discussed in this section, there are other fees associated with owning and using a credit card. We look at other fees because it is possible that, in an effort to recover lost penalty fee revenue, issuers may have raised these other fees. Such fees include debt suspension fees for consumers who elect to purchase a debt suspension product in conjunction with their account, balance transfer and cash advance fees for consumers who elect to make such transactions, and returned payment fees for consumers whose payment does not clear their bank. The largest dollar amount of other fees comes from debt suspension, which comprises about 45% of all other fees. Balance transfer fees represent approximately 25% of other fees and cash advance fees represent another 20%.

The decline in the incidence rate of other fees has been driven mostly by fewer accounts paying debt suspension fees. The number of accounts paying debt suspension fees declined significantly from 2008 to 2009 during the financial crisis and again in 2012. The significant decline in debt suspension fees in the fourth quarter of 2012 may be attributable to CFPB enforcement actions. The incidence rates of both balance transfer fees and cash advance fees fell in 2008 but have remained relatively steady since.

Total other fees declined from $2.0 billion per quarter in 2008 to $1.1 billion per quarter in 2012, albeit on a shrinking portfolio. On a per-active account basis, other fees *rose* from $1.35 per-active account per quarter in 2008 to $1.75 per-active account per quarter in 2012. Additional detail on other fees can be found in Appendix B in this report.

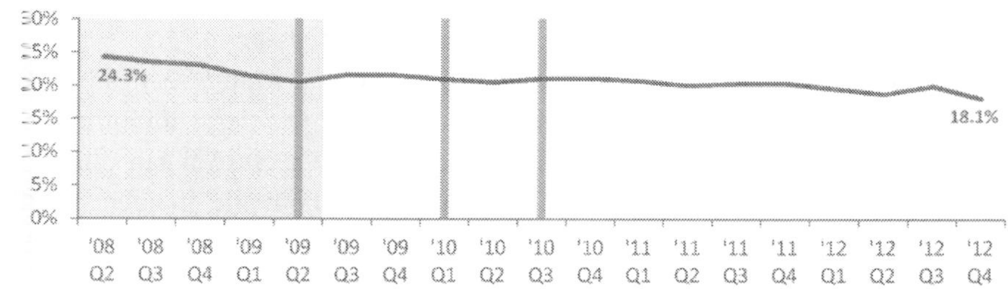

Source: CCDB; incidents of other fees divided by active accounts

Figure 5. Quarterly Incidence Rate of Other Fees (Active Accounts).

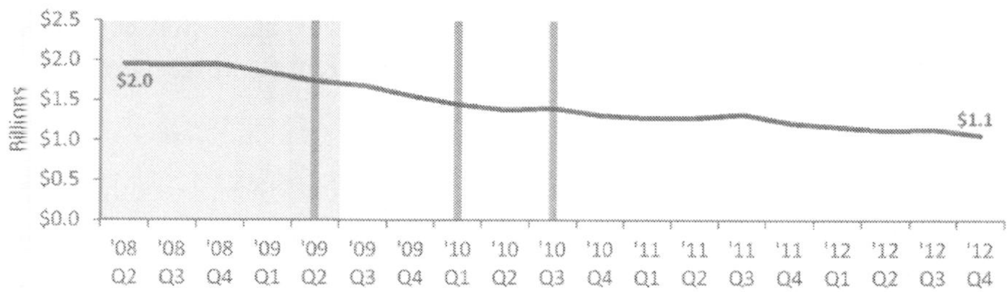

Source: CCDB.

Figure 6. Total Other Fees.

2.2.5. Repricing

Prior to the CARD Act, consumers were subject to changes in the APR on their credit card accounts on both existing balances and new transactions. For example, cardholder agreements established a "penalty APR" and permitted the issuer to increase the interest rate on an account up to the penalty APR if the consumer engaged in certain behavior. Often, these triggers included not only delinquency on the account governed by the agreement, but also delinquency on any of the consumer's other accounts (a practice known as "universal default"). Additionally, cardholder agreements generally contained a provision permitting the issuer to increase the interest rate at any time and for any reason. Per these provisions, many issuers periodically reassessed the risk of their accounts and changed the terms by raising interest rates on accounts that were considered more likely to default.

The CARD Act sharply curtailed repricing practices. Most importantly, the Act strictly limits the circumstances in which an interest rate increase can be applied to existing balances.[46] The Act also generally contains disclosure requirements before the rate can be increased on new transactions (or on existing balances) and review requirements at six-month intervals after rates are increased.[47]

To assess the impact of these changes, it is necessary to determine an appropriate baseline. As previously noted, in May 2008 the Board and other agencies issued proposed UDAP rules that would have limited the ability of issuers to increase the interest rate on existing balances.[48] That proposal may have led some issuers to reprice accounts while it was still lawful to do so. For that reason, and also because of the effect of the financial crisis that affected issuer behavior at the same time, the 2008 data in the CCDB may reflect an already elevated amount of repricing activity in the baseline. With these limitations in mind, we use 2008 as our baseline for assessing the change in repricing activity.

It is worth noting that, at the CARD Act Conference sponsored by the Bureau in 2011, Argus Information & Advisory Services presented data, drawn from large card issuers, which showed the incidence of repricing beginning in the third quarter of 2007.* The Argus data indicate that during the

* Repricing in the Argus presentation is defined as any upward repricing of retail APRs during the quarter. The magnitude of the repricing must be greater than 100 basis points and the retail APRs prior to the repricing action must be higher than 9.99%. The CFPB used a more comprehensive measure of repricing activity that includes all changes in terms, expiration of promotional APRs, and penalty APR. *Presentation available at* http://files.consumer finance.gov/f/2011/03/Argus-Presentation.pdf.

third and fourth quarters of 2007 and the first two quarters of 2008, the percentage of active accounts that were repriced each quarter was between 3.8% and 4.4%, with a quarterly average of 4.2% or an annual average of 16.8%. The incidence of rate increases began to rise in the third quarter of 2008 (perhaps in reaction to the proposed UDAP rules as well as deteriorating economic conditions) and continued at an elevated level through the first quarter of 2010 when the provisions of the CARD Act with respect to repricing took effect. Argus data looked only at penalty repricing, and included some definitional differences that are not reflected in our data. As a result, these numbers are not directly comparable.

As shown below, the incidence of repricing has declined to a quarterly rate of 1.5% in the year 2012 from 6.4% in the year 2008 (and from 4.2% in 2007 as shown by Argus, though again, this number is not directly comparable). That said, compared with prior periods we studied, the incidence of repricing has come down significantly. This allows us to determine that, although the exact magnitude of the decline is difficult to measure due to challenges with the initial baseline, the incidence of APR repricing has declined meaningfully, and has remained at very low levels since the CARD Act's February 2010 effective date of limitations on repricing activity.

We cannot answer the counter-factual question of what the incidence rate of pricing adjustments would have been in the absence of the CARD Act. For example, given the shift of the mix of accounts that has occurred over the past several years, a smaller percentage of accounts may have triggered a penalty repricing in 2012 than in 2007. What is clear, however, is that just as the CARD Act effectively eliminated overlimit fees, the restrictions on interest rate changes have substantially curtailed the issuer practice of changing interest rates on credit cards.

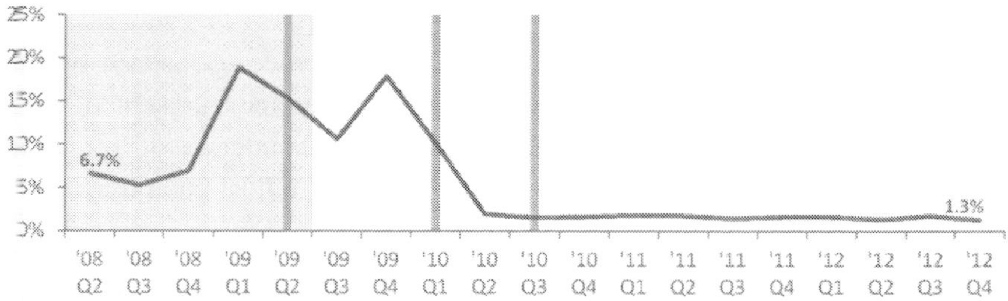

Source: CCDB.

Figure 7. Incidence Rate of Upwards APR Repricing (Active Accounts).

2.2.6. Retail APR and Effective Interest Rates

Except with respect to the repricing of accounts, the CARD Act did not directly regulate interest rates. Nonetheless, by affecting other components of pricing, the Act likely indirectly impacted the interest rate component of pricing.

Discussions of credit card interest rates often focus on the Annual Percentage Rate as it is the interest rate charged on balances (the "retail APR"). The APR is often used as shorthand for expressing the costs associated with using a credit card. However, for several reasons, the retail APR may not provide an accurate indication of the effective interest rates paid by consumers. The effective interest rate is defined as total interest charges for a period of time, stated as a percent of average cycle-ending balance for the same period of time.

As a general rule, interest charges are not assessed on an account so long as the consumer pays the balance in full each month by the due date. Thus, for many accounts the interest rate is not a meaningful measure of the cost of credit. For purposes of this report, we define a "transactor" account as an account where the balance is paid in full in two consecutive months. Based on the CCDB data, we find that 25%-30% of accounts required to make a payment pay off their balances in full for two consecutive months. For these transactor accounts, the primary cost is the annual fee. Consumers who do not expect to pay interest charges may not be rate sensitive, and thus the retail interest rate on these transactors' accounts may not be an important consideration in determining the interest costs for consumers who are actually paying interest.

Furthermore, it is quite common for a credit card account to have multiple APRs for different types of balances. For example, some accounts may have a promotional ("teaser") rate for a period of time. For newly-originated accounts, the promotional rate may apply to purchases, to transferred balances, or to both. For existing accounts, promotional rates generally are offered only on newly-transferred balances. Additionally, if a consumer uses a credit card account to obtain cash from an ATM or a bank teller, there is generally a "cash advance APR" which will be significantly higher than the purchase APR. And, as we have seen, prior to the CARD Act, a significant percentage of accounts were charged a penalty APR.

It is important to note that, where an account has different balances at different interest rates, the order in which payments are applied to these various balances will impact the effective interest rate over time. This is one of the areas regulated by the CARD Act as payments are now required to be applied to balances with the highest interest rate first (with limited exceptions).

We first examine the retail APR on accounts in the CCDB.* We find that, beginning in the first quarter of 2009 and continuing through the second quarter of 2010, the first full quarter after most of the provisions of the CARD Act took effect, the account-weighted average retail APR† increased by 230 basis points, rising from 16.2% to 18.5 %. The increase was more modest among accounts with deep subprime credit scores (140 basis points) and highest among accounts with prime (280 basis points) and superprime (260 basis points) credit scores. Interest rates stabilized and drifted slightly downward thereafter, dropping 10 basis points on an aggregate basis (to 18.4%) with accounts with superprime credit scores showing a slight increase and other tiers showing decreases.

While there are a number of factors which could explain the interest rate increases observed in the 2009 and early 2010 time frame (including, for example, the migration of accounts from one risk tier to another), these increases are consistent with the observations previously made in this report with respect to the impact of the rising charge-offs that issuers were experiencing and with the issuers' desire to adjust pricing ahead of regulatory changes that would impact their ability to do so.

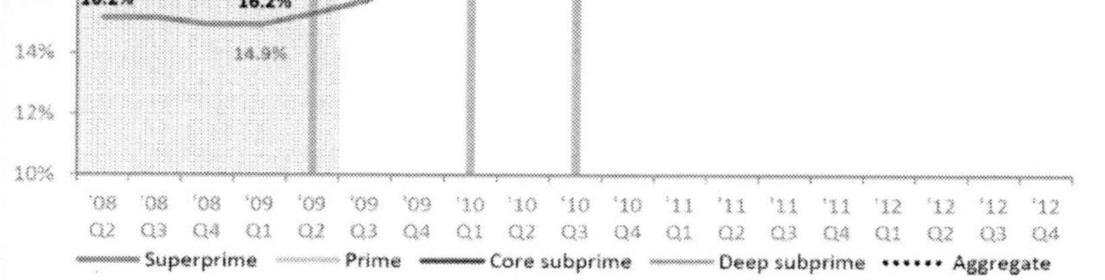

Source: CCDB; note: Y-axis does not start at zero.

Figure 8. Average Retail APR (Open Accounts).

* Prime, the underlying index that is used as the basis for pricing credit cards, fell to 3.25% in 2008, and remained flat at 3.25% through 2012. As a result, the underlying benchmark was not a factor in changing APRs on credit cards.

† The account-weighted average retail APR is calculated based on all of the accounts in the quarter for every month in the quarter.

Figure 9 shows the effective interest rate for accounts carrying a balance and by risk tier.

The retail APR for revolving accounts increased by 230 basis points from Q4 2008 to Q4 2012, but the effective interest rate remained flat for the same time period. For accounts with deep subprime credit scores, the effective interest rate fell by 200 basis points from Q4 2008 to Q4 2012, with much of that decline occurring during the period prior to when most of the CARD Act provisions became effective in February 2010 when retail interest rates were increasing. The effective interest rate in other parts of the credit spectrum rose as well, but at a much slower pace than the retail APR.

2.3. Total Cost of Credit

To capture the all-in cost of credit, the Bureau has developed a Total Cost of Credit metric ("TCC") that expresses the totality of payments from consumers to issuers as a percentage of average cycle-ending balance. The TCC is calculated quarterly and annualized, and can be applied to any group of accounts. Because of seasonal variations in consumer (and potentially issuer) behavior, point-in-time comparisons can be skewed. However, by looking at the average annualized TCC over comparable time periods, meaningful trends can be detected.

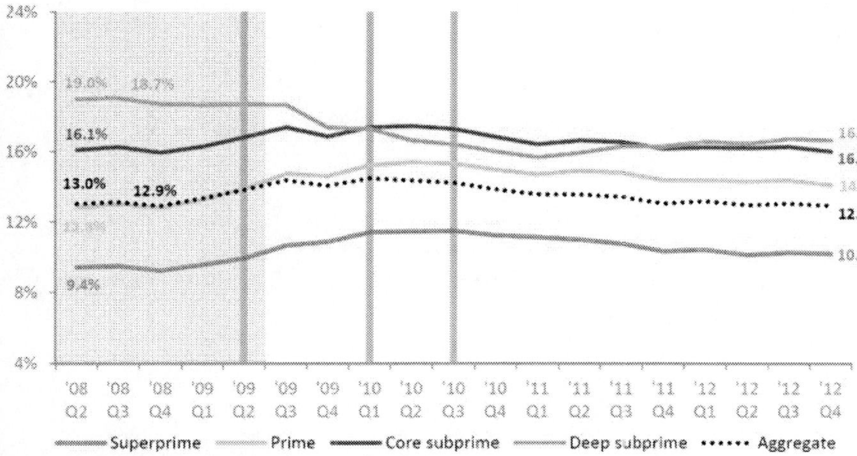

Source: CCDB; note: Y-axis does not start at zero.

Figure 9. Effective Interest Rate (Revolving Accounts).

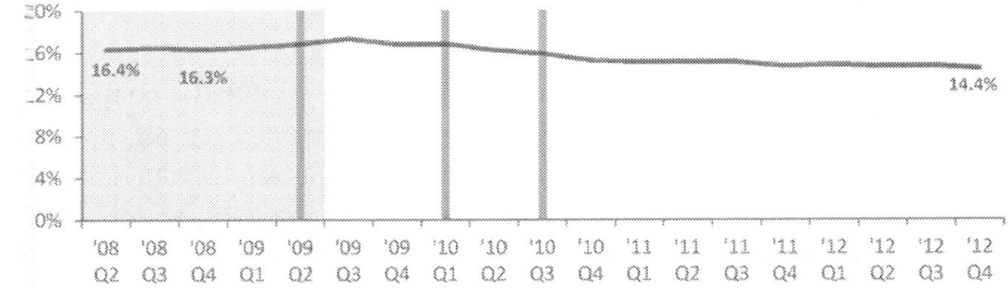

Source: CCDB; all interest charges and fees divided by average balance.

Figure 10. Total Cost of Credit (% of Average Cycle Ending Balance, All Consumers, Annualized).

Figure 10 shows that the Total Cost of Credit declined by 190 basis points from Q4 2008 to Q4 2012, driven by the decline in late and overlimit fees mentioned earlier. The decline was partially offset by an increase in annual and other fees.

As mentioned earlier, our data shows that 25%–30% of active accounts pay off their balances in full for two consecutive months. These accounts are classified as transactors. The remaining active accounts carry a balance from month to month all or most of the time. These accounts are classified as "revolvers." In our data, some accounts are classified as revolving, even if they sometimes paid in full at the end of the month. Revolvers comprise nearly 90% of the credit card balances in the CCDB and pay the bulk of all fees and interest charges. Therefore, it is useful to further examine TCC among revolvers.

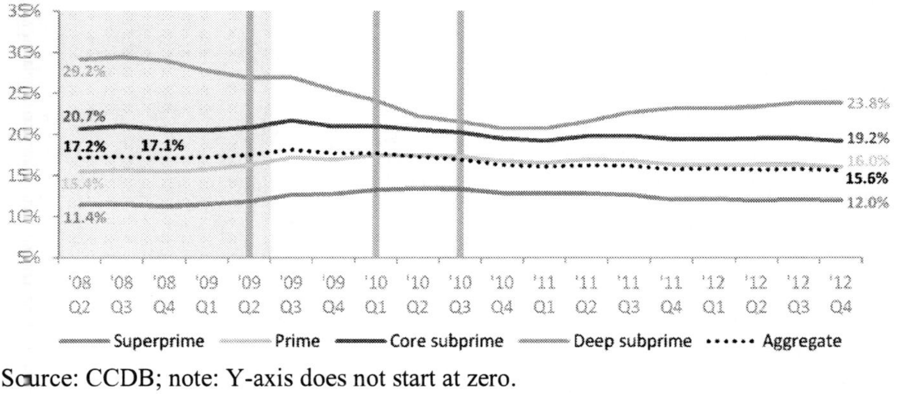

Source: CCDB; note: Y-axis does not start at zero.

Figure 11. Total Cost of Credit (% of average cycle ending balance, revolving accounts, annualized).

The TCC for revolvers follows the same aggregate pattern as for the entire set of accounts, increasing from 2008 to 2009 and then steadily declining thereafter. On an aggregate basis, TCC for revolvers declined by 150 basis points from Q4 2008 to Q4 2012.

A key driver in the decline for revolvers in the TCC is fee revenue. Total fees as a percentage of outstanding balance are 180 basis points lower in Q4 2010 compared to Q4 2008 as shown in Figure 12 below.

This is not meant to indicate that the decrease in the TCC is attributable to the CARD Act. The TCC as we have defined it reflects an interaction of the terms and pricing practices on credit card accounts, the manner in which consumers use those accounts, the manner in which issuers choose to assess fees or adjust terms where permitted by cardholder agreements, and the mix of consumers who have accounts. For example, if consumers with accounts in 2012 were more careful to make payments on time than consumers with accounts in 2008, that will result in a reduction in late fee incidence and thus a decline in the TCC; indeed, at least a portion of the decline in fees resulted from the fall in delinquencies from their Great Recession highs in 2008. Similarly, if consumers increase their monthly payments, this will drive down their TCC due in part to changes in the application of payments required by the CARD Act. Thus, the potential interaction of the CARD Act with other factors is complex and difficult to disentangle.

2.4. Comparisons to Other Credit Markets

Next, we examine the counter-factual question: might the cost of credit have come down even further were it not for the CARD Act?

One way to shed light on that question is to compare trends in credit costs in the consumer credit card marketplace with trends in other domestic credit markets which were not subject to CARD Act regulation. Such comparisons are inherently uncertain. Different credit markets use different sources of funding, have different cost structures including loan losses, and have different demand dynamics, among other things. These factors do not necessarily move in parallel across credit markets. Thus, even if all regulation were held constant for the different credit markets, it is not clear that the costs of credit would move together for those markets. Despite these limitations, we have examined the cost of credit in the small business credit card market, as described in the methodology section of this review, and compared trends in that market with trends in the consumer credit card market.

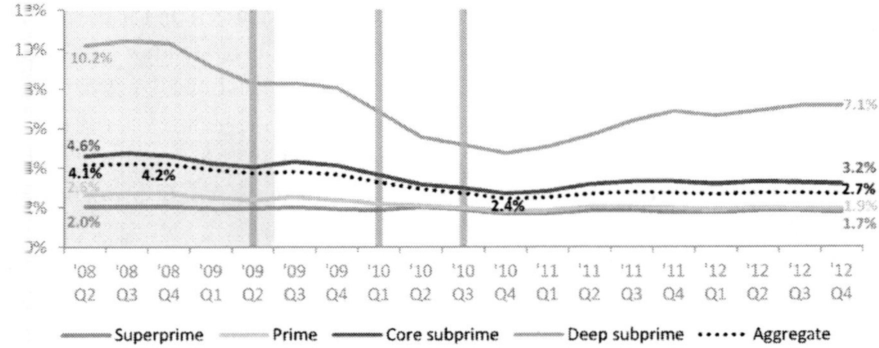

Source: CCDB.

Figure 12. Fees (% of Average Cycle Ending Balance, Revolving Accounts, Annualized).

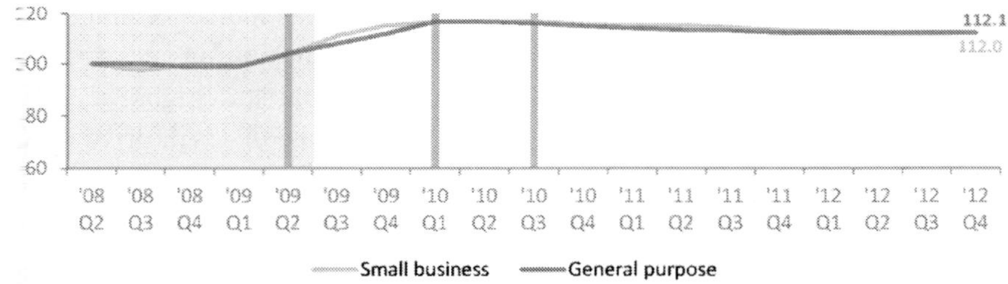

Source: CCDB; note: Y-axis does not start at zero.

Figure 13. Average Retail Apr – General Purpose vs. Small Business (Indexed to 100 in Q2 2008, Revolving Accounts).

If the CARD Act had retarded the rate of reduction of credit costs in the consumer marketplace, we might expect to see sharper reductions in credit costs in the small business marketplace than in the consumer market. The data, however, does not show such a pattern or support such an assertion.

We first examine the retail APR on small business cards in the CCDB. Similar to consumer cards, small business cards also experienced an increase in retail APR starting in the second quarter of 2009, and the interest rate trend is nearly identical.

When we switch our focus from retail APR to TCC, we see that the TCC for consumer accounts fell more than for small business cards. The chart below looks at the TCC for revolvers in the two markets, and shows that TCC for consumers declined by 10.0% overall from Q2 2008 to Q4 2012, while TCC for small business cards rose by 3.7%. While there are many moving parts in each of these portfolios (including composition shifts), the difference noted here suggests that the CARD Act likely did not raise credit card costs for consumers.

2.5. Conclusion

The CARD Act has likely impacted the component costs of credit cards in a way that has significantly enhanced transparency for consumers. Overlimit fees and repricing actions have been largely eliminated; those effects can be directly traced to the Act. The dollar amount per late fee is down as well and the incidence rate is down from 2008-2009 levels although it remains at or above 2007 levels.

The end result is a market in which the costs incurred by consumers are driven more by APR and annual fees and less by back-end penalty fees and APR repricing. For consumers looking for a credit card, comparison shopping is far more straightforward than it was prior to the enactment of the Act. Similarly, consumers deciding whether to finance a purchase with an existing account can make that decision with far more confidence that the cost of financing will be a function of their current interest rate rather than some yet-to-be-determined interest rate that could be reassessed at any time and for any reason by the issuer.

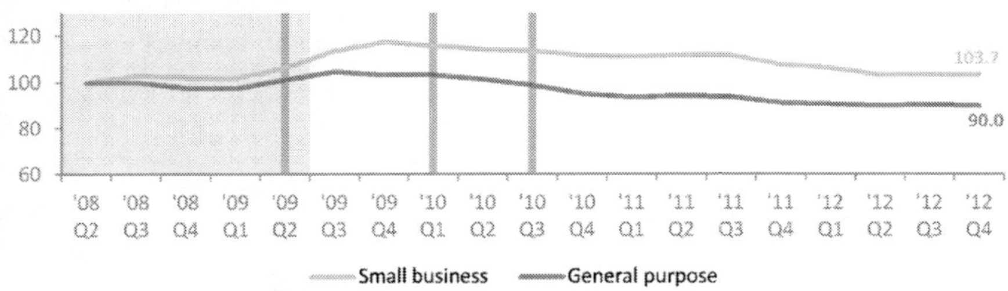

Source: CCDB; note: Y-axis does not start at zero.

Figure 14. Total Cost of Credit – General Purpose vs. Small Business (Indexed to 100 in Q2 2008, Revolving Accounts).

Assessing the impact of the CARD Act on the Total Cost of Credit is more complex. There clearly was an increase in interest rates and in the TCC during the year leading up to the date that most of the CARD Act provisions became effective (February 2010) and a decline since then, with a net reduction in the Total Cost of Credit of approximately 190 basis points. Further research is required to assess how much of that decrease can be attributable to the Act.

3. Availability of Credit

3.1. Introduction

The main purpose of this section is to analyze the availability of credit and assess whether there are changes in the availability of credit that can be attributed to the CARD Act. As we have seen, some of the provisions of the CARD Act regulate the circumstances in which credit may be extended. Thus, in assessing the availability of credit here and asking whether there has been a change, we do not intend to imply that the level of credit availability that prevailed prior to the CARD Act was socially optimal or to render any judgments as to the optimal level of credit availability in the credit card marketplace.

Assessing credit availability is a challenging task. The most readily available measures – such as the total amount of credit line on credit card accounts, the total number of accounts, or the number of new accounts originated– conflate the willingness of issuers to make credit available to consumers (supply) and the willingness of consumers to avail themselves of the credit that issuers are willing to extend (demand). Even measures of marketing activity, such as mail solicitations volume, are impacted by demand as well as supply since marketing is likely to fall when there is weak demand. Because the availability of credit is difficult to evaluate using a single metric, we look at a variety of metrics in order to estimate changes in credit availability.

3.2. Supply and Demand

3.2.1. Overall Solicitations

Traditionally, credit card issuers used mail solicitations to prospective applicants as their principal means of originating new accounts. Most often, these mailings were pre-screened or pre-approved, meaning that the names of the prospects had been obtained from, or run through, a credit reporting agency and a determination was made that the prospects likely met the issuer's credit criteria for issuing an account. For these reasons, mail solicitation volume has often been viewed as a proxy for credit availability, but it is a crude measure for several reasons. The number of solicitations an issuer mails in any given period of time is a function of the issuer's marketing budget and decisions the issuer makes to allocate that budget across various alternative marketing channels. Those decisions, in turn, rest on the issuer's assessment of the relative cost effectiveness of alternative channels. It is not the case that issuers regularly mail all of the prospects that would be eligible for credit if they were to apply. Thus, mail volume is not necessarily a good indicator of the number of consumers to whom an issuer is willing to extend credit, and changes in mail volume may be attributable to factors wholly unrelated to changes in credit availability such, as for example, increases in postage cost or the development of new marketing channels such as social media. Nonetheless, because mail solicitation volume is a metric often referenced in connection with credit availability, we begin by analyzing mail solicitation trends, using estimates developed by Mintel Comperemedia. Mintel maintains a panel of consumers that provide copies of the solicitations they receive, from which Mintel estimates aggregate national mail volume.

According to Mintel, from 2007 through mid-2009 credit card mail volume declined significantly.

Mail volume reached its low in July 2009 at 18.9% of the July 2007 level. The first major implementation date of the CARD Act (February 2010) coincided with a modest rebound in mail volume, and mail volumes continued to rise thereafter, reaching 70.5% of 2007 levels by July of 2011. Interestingly, starting in late 2011 – almost two years after the CARD Act took effect -- mail volume began to trend down again and in July of 2012 reached 37.0% of the 2007 level, which may reflect the growing importance of alternative channels such as online communications and social media.

3.2.2. New Account Originations

A second possible metric for evaluating credit availability is the number of new accounts being originated. This, too, is an imperfect measure since new accounts are a function of the intersection of consumer demand for credit and issuers' willingness to issue credit to those who apply.

The chart below shows trends in new account originations since 2007 for general purpose credit cards that can be used anywhere the card network (e.g. Visa and MasterCard) is accepted, and private label credit cards, which can generally be used only at a particular merchant. The data is derived from the CCPI, which allows us to look at trends since 2007 for issuers representing approximately 80% of the market by outstandings.

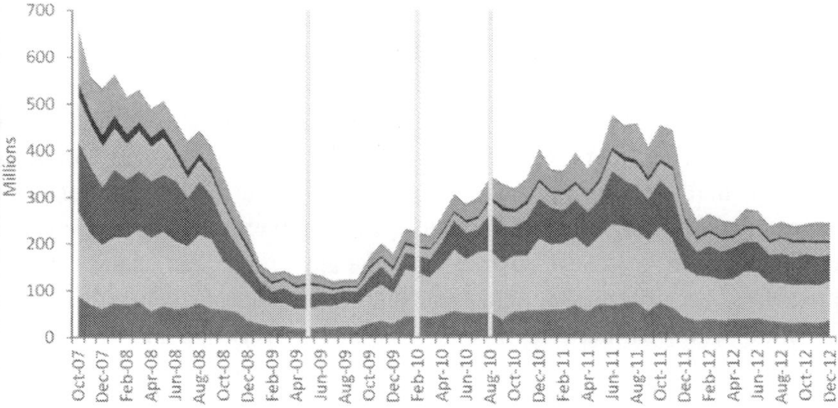

Source: Mintel Comper*.

Figure 15. Mail Volume Trends.

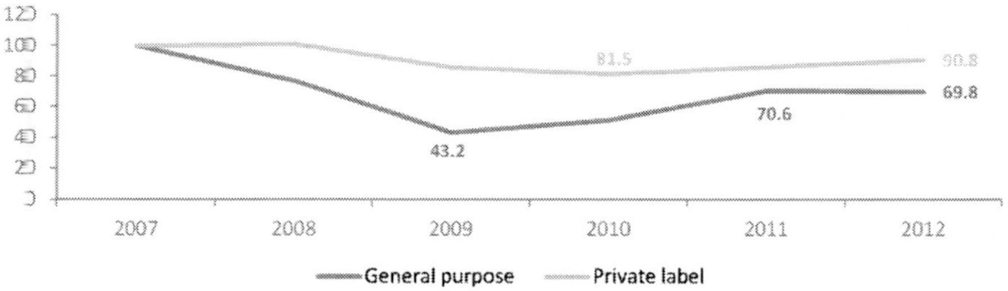

Source: CCPI.

Figure 16. New Account Origination Volume (Indexed to 100 in 2007).

As the chart shows, new account origination volume for general purpose credit cards declined from 2007 through 2009, bottoming out at 43.2% of the 2007 (pre-recession) level. The end of the recession and the implementation of the CARD Act coincided with a rebound in originations, reaching 70.6% of the 2007 level in 2011 and 69.8% in 2012.

* A set of widely used risk scores developed by credit reporting agencies to assess a consumer's creditworthiness. VantageScores can range from 501 to 990 (though in 2013, a new VantageScore scale was introduced that ranges from 300 to 850). The VantageScore scale can be mapped to letter grades from A to F, where F represents the highest risk of default. The score range translates to letter grades as follows: 901-990 = A or Super Prime, 801-900 = B or Prime Plus, 701-800 = C or Prime, 601-700 = D or Non-Prime, and 501-600 = F or High Risk.

Private label originations have followed a somewhat different trajectory. Originations of these accounts declined through 2010 (rather than through 2009), but at a more modest pace than in the general purpose credit card market, bottoming out at 81.5% of 2007 levels. Since 2010, there has been a recovery and originations in 2012 were 90.8% of 2007 levels.

3.2.3. Subprime Solicitations and New Accounts

From 2007-2009, mail volume in the subprime market (VantageScore bands D and F) declined more severely than in the overall market, dropping in October 2009 to 17.7% of October 2007 levels (as compared to 26.0% for all mail volume, including subprime). Interestingly, however, whereas mail volume increased sharply through 2011 as the economy recovered, subprime volume was relatively flat and increased only slightly in October 2011 to 35.7% of October 2007 levels (as compared to 69.0% for all mail volume). Mail volume in the subprime market declined in October 2012 to 23.1% of October 2007 levels. This suggests there has been a meaningful pullback from mail in the subprime credit card space.

The new account originations of accounts with subprime credit scores for the issuers who provided data in response to the CCPI is shown in Figure 17. Due to data limitations, in this section we refer to subprime as FICO <660, as we do not have the detail to look at deep subprime separate from core subprime; we use the score at the point of origination.

For general purpose credit cards, subprime originations bottomed out in 2009 at 21.2% of 2007 levels (compared to 43.2% for the overall market including subprime). Subprime originations turned upward in 2010, reaching 63.0% of 2007 levels in 2011 before dipping slightly in 2012; this compares with a recovery to 70.6% of 2007 levels for the overall market, including subprime.

For private label cards, subprime originations declined in 2008 and 2009 to 43.4% of 2007 levels; this is a much sharper decline that was seen in the overall market (which bottomed out at 81.5% of 2007 levels). Subprime private label originations rebounded beginning in 2010 and reached 70.3% of 2007 levels in 2012 (well below the results for the overall private label originations, which reached 90.8% of 2007 levels). The decline in origination volume suggests a reduction in availability of credit for customers with subprime scores.

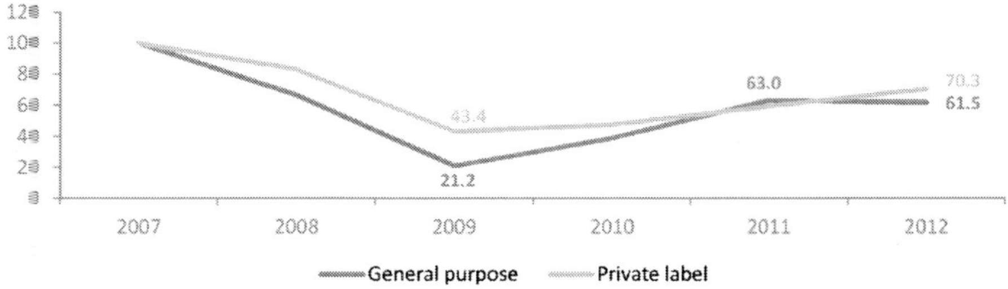

Source: CCPI.

Figure 17. Subprime New Account Origination Volume (Indexed to 100 in 2007).

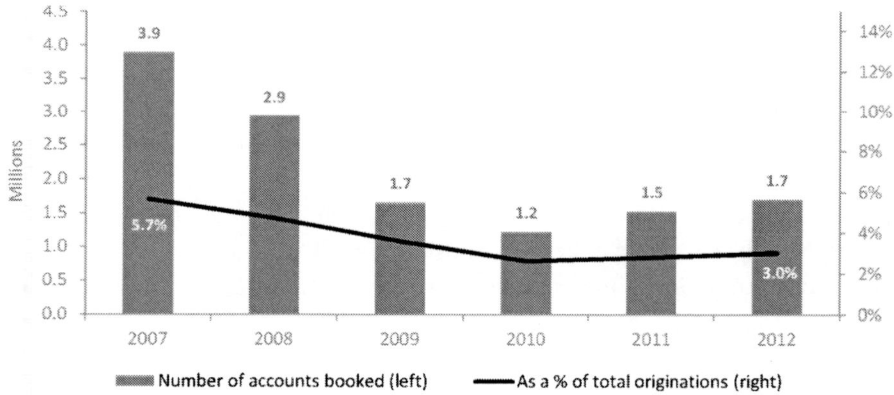

Source: CCPI.

Figure 18. New Cards Issued To Cardholders Under Age 21.

3.2.4. New Accounts for Students and Young Adults

The CARD Act included several provisions designed to protect young consumers and reform the way credit cards are marketed and issued to students. The Act prohibits the marketing of pre-approved offers to a consumer under the age of 21 without the consumer's consent.[49] It also prohibited the issuance of credit cards to consumers under the age of 21 without a written application demonstrating the applicant's independent ability to make payments on the account or a cosigner age of 21 or over with the means to make payments.[50, 51] The Act further limited issuers' ability to market credit cards to students on or near campus and at school-sponsored events by prohibiting the use of gifts or any tangible items to induce students to apply for credit cards.[52]

Issuer responses to our CCPI show the overall number of new cards for consumers under the age of 21 has decreased significantly since pre-crisis years to just 43.5% of 2007 levels. In this sense, less credit is available to students and young adults than in the past. While some of this may be attributable to the recession, this reduction in accounts among the student and young adult population may be viewed as consistent with congressional intent for the CARD Act.

An analysis of the age at which young adults receive their first credit cards reveals a similar story. Drawn from the Bureau's Consumer Credit Panel, the figure below shows the proportion of consumers 18-20 with at least one credit card.

The figure reveals that there was a pronounced decline in card ownership for consumers age 18- 20 after the CARD Act's provisions relating to consumers age 18-20 were implemented in February 2010. There is a markedly lower rate of credit cards among consumers under the age of 21 in 2010 and beyond compared to the 2006 - 2008 level. The decline started in 2009, prior to the CARD Act implementation date, and that may indicate some impact from the Great Recession as well. This data provides further evidence that the CARD Act has restricted the availability of credit to students and young adults.

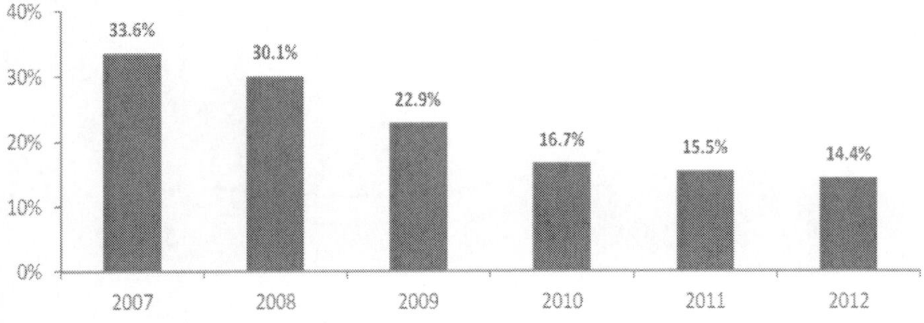

Source: CFPB Consumer Credit Panel.

Figure 19. % of Consumers Ages 18–20 Who Have Opened a Credit Card Account.

3.2.5. New Account Originations Across Consumer Credit Markets

By using the metric of new originations to look at credit availability in the credit card marketplace, we are able to draw comparisons with other consumer credit markets and to examine whether the consumer credit card market – which was the only market affected by the CARD Act – is an outlier. As we have previously discussed, the best point of comparison for the consumer credit card market is the market for small business credit cards.

The chart below shows new account originations as reported by Experian and Oliver Wyman in quarterly Market Intelligence Reports produced from a nationally representative random sample of credit reports.

What is most striking in this figure is the difference in performance across different credit markets. The market for home equity loans and lines of credit experienced a sharp decline in new accounts between 2007 and 2009 and has basically remained level since then.

The market for auto loans and leases experienced a similar although less steep decline and a sharp recovery such that 2012 originations exceeded originations in 2007. Credit card originations lie squarely in the middle of product origination trends, suggesting that the card marketplace is not an outlier as a result of the CARD Act.

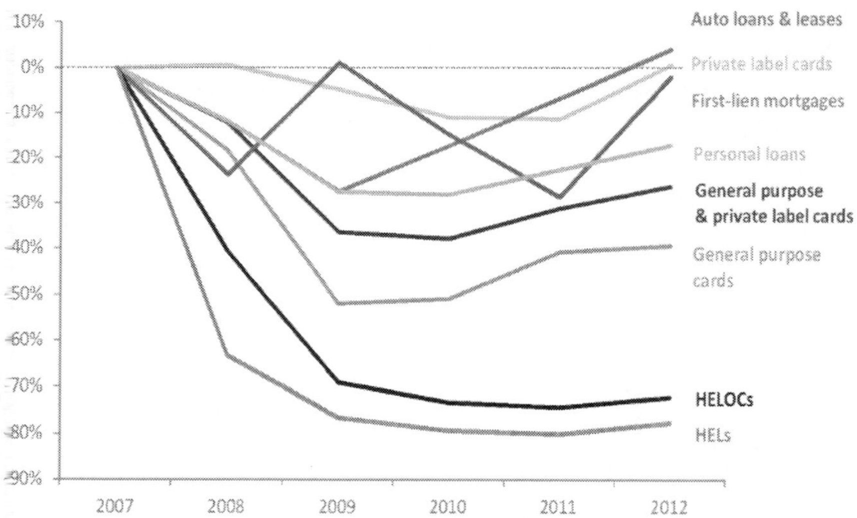

Source: Oliver Wyman/Experian Market Intelligence*.

Figure 20. New Account Originations by Product (% Change from 2007).

* There is a known issue within the Oliver Wyman/Experian Market Intelligence data to note. During Q1 and Q2 of 2007, one private label card issuer failed to report data and is therefore missing from the data set. Despite this data discrepancy, quarterly private label card origination data into 2013 and data from the Credit Card Practices Inquiry lead us to the conclusion that private label card originations have rebounded significantly since 2007.

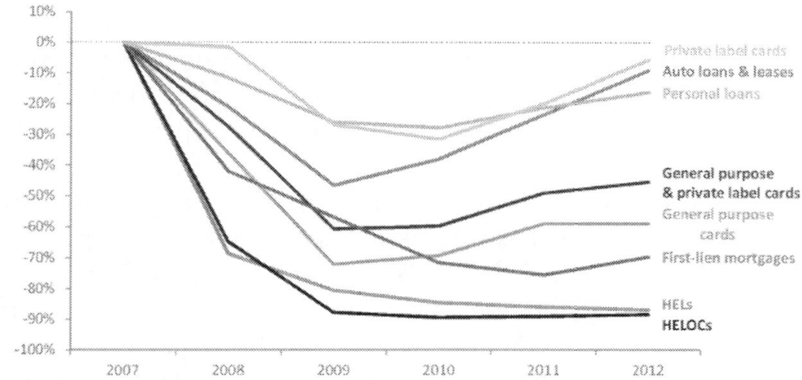

Source: Oliver Wyman/Experian Market Intelligence Data.

Figure 21. New Account Originations by Product (% Change From 2007, Vantagescores D & F)*.

Focusing on the subprime market reveals a similar pattern. For all markets, subprime originations in 2012 were below 2007 levels but the extent of the variance differs widely across markets with auto lending and private label cards leading the pack in terms of recovery. As shown below in Figure 21, general purpose credit cards appear to reside in the middle of the pack. The notable difference is that subprime credit cards recovered more than subprime first lien mortgages. As in the overall market, nothing here suggests that subprime credit cards are an outlier due to the CARD Act.

3.2.6. Approval Rates

Approval rates – the percentage of applications approved for an extension of credit -- are a more direct way of assessing credit availability than looking at either mail volume or origination volume. But even this metric must be approached with caution since there are a variety of other factors that can affect changes in approval rates. For example, within any given risk tier there can be a change in the application mix over time, which could result in changes in approval rates unrelated to any change in credit criteria. Additionally, changes in the channel through which applications are received can result in changes in approval rates, as would be expected, for example, if the percentage of pre-approved applications declined over time. Thus, even approval rates are an imperfect measure of credit availability.

* A set of widely used risk scores developed by credit reporting agencies to assess a consumer's creditworthiness. VantageScores 601-700 = D or Non-Prime, and 501-600 = F or High Risk.

In contrast to mail volume and origination volume data, which can be procured from commercial sources, data with respect to approval rates is more difficult to obtain. However, the issuers participating in the Bureau's Credit Card Practices Inquiry provided data to the Bureau for the period from 2007 to 2012, as shown in Figure 22 below.

Consistent with the trends observed in mail volume and applications, in each of the risk ranges and in the aggregate, approval rates for general purpose credit cards declined from 2007 to 2009 with the onset of the financial crisis. The decline was modest in the superprime segment, with approval rates dropping from 92.0% to 80.7%, a 12.3% decline. In the prime segment, the drop was much sharper, from 74.6% to 44.9%, a 39.8% decline. And in the subprime segment, approval rates dropped from 23.1% to 9.6%, a 58.4% decline.

In the subprime and prime segments, approval rates began to recover in 2010 with the economic recovery (coincident with the implementation of the CARD Act) and by 2012 had reached 74% and 78.7% of the 2007 levels, respectively. In the superprime segment, approval rates turned up in 2011 and by 2012 had reached 92.9% of the 2007 level.

The approval rates for private label cards experienced a decline in the aggregate and in the prime and superprime segments from 2007 to 2010, but to a lesser extent than general purpose cards.

The subprime segment experienced the most significant decline out of the three score ranges, falling from 31.1% in 2007 to 15.8% in 2009.

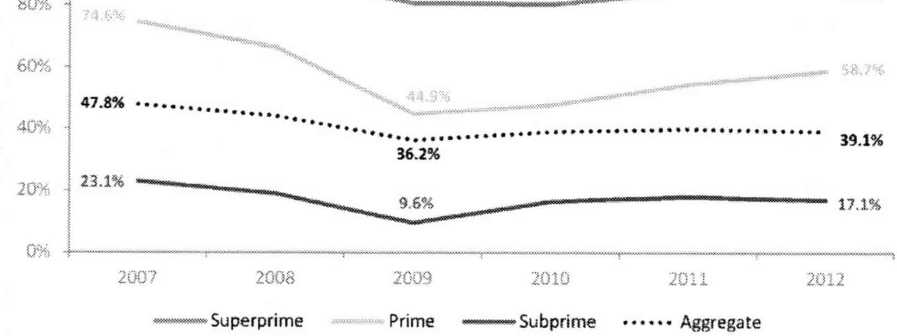

Source: CCPI.

Figure 22. Approval Rate for General Purpose Cards.

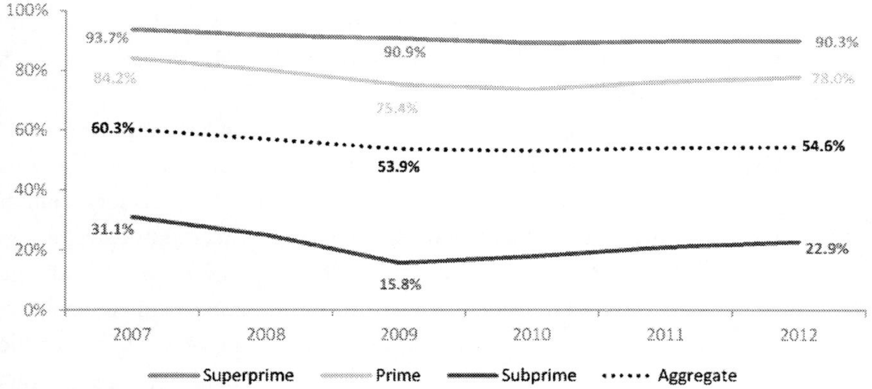

Source: CCPI.

Figure 23. Approval Rate for Private Label Cards.

The approval rates for superprime and prime began to recover in 2011. By 2012, the approval rate had recovered to 96.4% of 2007 levels for the superprime segment and 92.6% of 2007 levels for the prime segment. The approval rate for subprime began recovering in 2010. As of 2012, the approval rate for subprime has recovered to 73.6% of the 2007 level.

While we note that approval rates have increased since the effective date of the CARD Act, based on issuer responses to the Bureau's CCPI, it appears that at least in one respect the CARD Act has depressed approval rates. The CARD Act and its implementing regulation requires issuers, before opening a credit card account or increasing a credit line on a card account for a consumer, to evaluate the consumer's ability to pay the credit. That evaluation is based upon the consumer's income or assets and the consumer's current obligations, such as the debt-to-income ratio or debt-to-asset ratio.[53] The issuers participating in the CCPI report that approximately 2% to 3% of their applicant pool met the issuers' credit criteria but were declined due to the criterion required by the ability-to-pay rules. Most issuers report that the impact of the ability-to-pay rules is largely on prime and/or superprime applicants, and is less of an issue in subprime segments. To the extent that the ability-to-pay rules have led to some decline in credit availability, that may be an intended consequence of the Act. Nonetheless, to reduce unintended consequences of the Act and its implementing regulations, in May 2013, the Bureau amended the ability-to-pay rules to address concerns that the rules unduly limited the ability of spouses and partners not working outside the home to obtain credit cards based on the income of the other spouse or partner.[54] The final rule removes the requirement that issuers consider the consumer's independent ability to pay for consumers who are 21 or older, and permits issuers to consider income and assets to which such consumers have a reasonable expectation of access.

In addition to containing a general ability-to-pay requirement, the CARD Act contains special requirements with respect to students and other persons under 21. Under the Act and its implementing regulations, issuers cannot extend credit to such individuals unless the applicant demonstrates an independent ability to pay, or provides a cosigner age 21 or over with the means to pay.[55] To the extent issuers received applications from consumers under age 21 who could not satisfy this test, they would be required under the Act to decline the applicant. We did not have the data to evaluate whether this factor limited the recovery in approval rates that occurred since 2010.

3.2.7. New Line Size

Yet another way to evaluate credit availability is to look at the amount of credit an issuer is willing to extend to a consumer who is approved for credit. For existing accounts, this is a problematic metric since the amount of credit that is extended to an existing customer will be influenced by the customer's prior behavior and utilization of credit previously extended. For new accounts, however, the size of the line extended provides a more useful measure of credit availability.

We were unable to obtain information on credit lines in the CCPI. However, from the CCDB we can examine line assignments, albeit starting in 2008 rather than in 2007 as shown below.

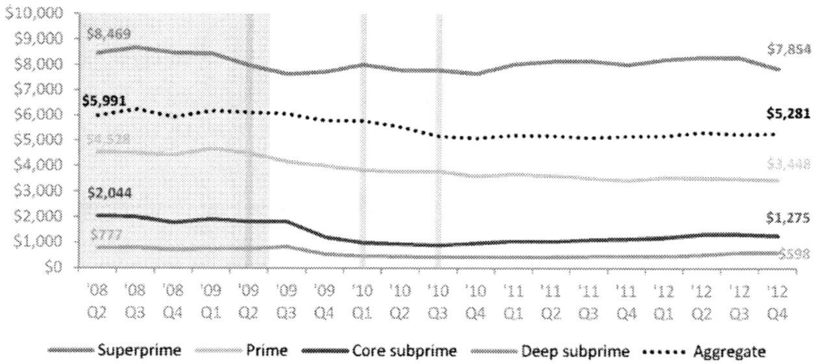

Source: CCDB.

Figure 24. Average Size of New Lines (General Purpose Cards).

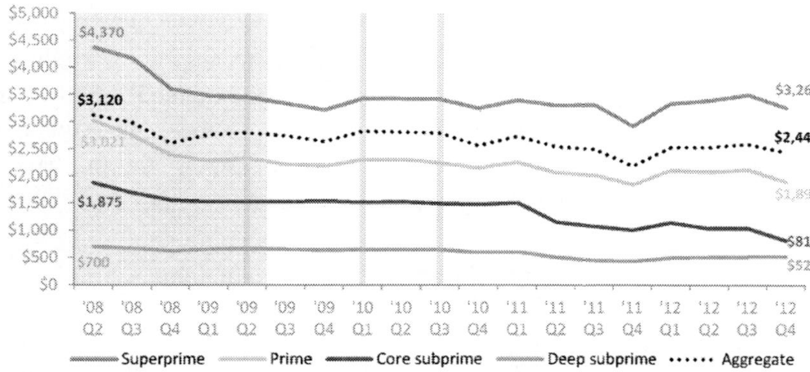

Source: CCDB.

Figure 25. Average Size of New Lines (Private Label Cards).

For general purpose credit cards, in the superprime and also the core subprime and deep subprime segments, the figure indicates that new line assignments decreased from the second quarter of 2008 through Q3 2009 (in the case of superprime) or Q3 2010 (in the case of the two subprime segments) and then reversed direction. In percentage terms, the decline was smallest in the superprime segment (where lines bottomed out at 90.2% of the Q2 2008 level) and greatest in core subprime (where lines bottomed out at 43.6% of Q2 2008 levels). By the end of 2012, line assignments in superprime were 92.7% of the baseline level, whereas in core subprime line assignments were 62.4% of the baseline level.

The trend in the prime segment was different, with line assignments increasing slightly in 2008 (by 3.3%) and steadily declining since. At the end of 2012, line assignments in this segment were 76.2% of Q2 2008 levels.

Line assignments on new private label accounts experienced a larger decline than did general purpose cards, falling by over 20% in aggregate. Again, core subprime new lines experienced the largest reduction through Q4 2012, reaching 43.7% of Q2 2008 levels. There is less indication of a recovery in the private label line assignments compared to the general purpose market.

3.3. Total Credit Line

Total credit line measures the amount of credit that issuers have extended to consumers, whether used or unused. It, too, is an imperfect measure of the availability of credit – that is, of the extent to which issuers are willing to extend credit – since the total amount of credit line is a product of the intersection of supply and demand. Nonetheless, because total credit line measures the aggregate amount of credit that has been extended (whether used or unused), a discussion of credit availability would be incomplete without a discussion of total credit line. Note that for this section, for the sake of simplicity, we combine general purpose and private label cards.

3.3.1. Time Series Overview of Total Extended Credit Line

Total Consumer Credit Line

For issuers in the CCDB, total credit line (whether used or unused) has experienced a considerable decline from $3.6 trillion in Q2 2008 to $2.4 trillion in Q4 2012, representing a 32.4% decrease. Approximately 60% of the $1.1 trillion in total line reductions occurred before passage of the CARD Act and almost 74% occurred before the implementation of the major provisions of the Act.

Accounts with superprime credit scores represent a disproportionate share of total line; this is to be expected since these accounts receive higher lines than accounts with lower credit scores. In addition to showing an overall decline in the total size of outstanding credit lines, Figure 26 reflects a change in the composition of those lines. In Q4 2012, 80.0% of total credit is available to superprime credit card accounts, compared with 73.8% of total line in Q2 2008. The total line for accounts with superprime credit scores declined by 26.7% over this time period. Over the same period, total credit line extended to accounts with deep subprime credit scores fell 54.3% from $142.2 billion to $65.0 billion. Combined subprime share of line fell from 8.1% to 6.0% over the period.

It is important to bear in mind that these analyses are based upon refreshed FICO scores. Thus, for example, to the extent individual consumers migrated from subprime to prime, the effect on our analysis would be to reduce the share of subprime lines and increase the share of prime lines. This limits the utility of the comparisons over time.

Unused Line

Despite the reductions in total credit line, consumers still have a significant, albeit declining, amount of unused credit line on their card accounts. From Q2 2008 to Q4 2012, total unused line fell by 35.0% yet at the end of 2012 consumers with accounts represented in the CCDB still enjoyed $1.9 trillion in available credit on their credit cards. This implies that 20.5% of the extended credit line has actually been utilized by consumers, up from 17.4% in Q2 2008 (some of this increase is seasonal as credit usage customarily increases during the holiday season).

Accounts with subprime credit scores experienced the biggest reductions, as core subprime and deep subprime saw reductions of 61.9% and 69.7%, respectively, from Q2 2008 to Q4 2012. Despite the decline in subprime unused line, it should be noted that there was still $38.6 billion in unused line available to consumers with subprime scores in Q4 2012.

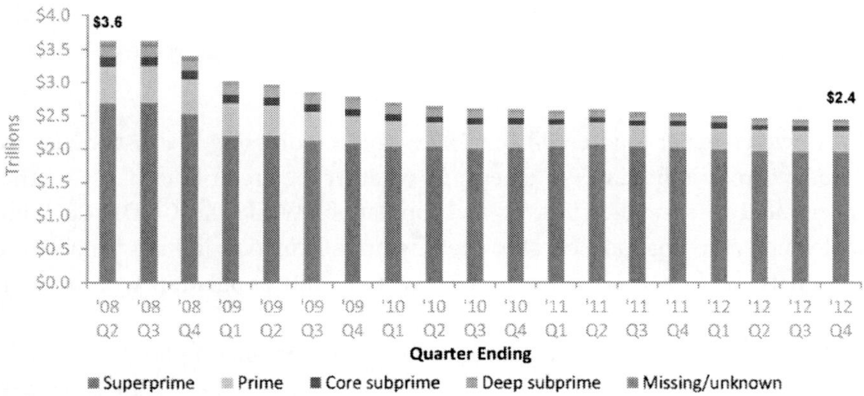

Source: CCDB.

Figure 26. Total Credit Line.

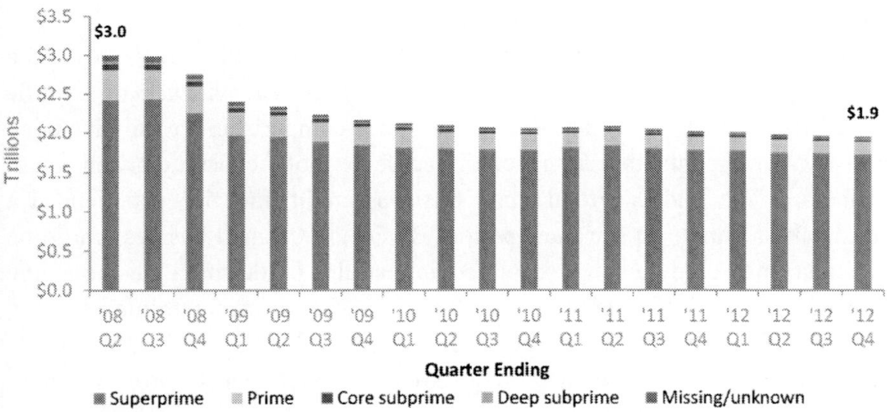

Source: CCDB.

Figure 27. Total Unused Line.

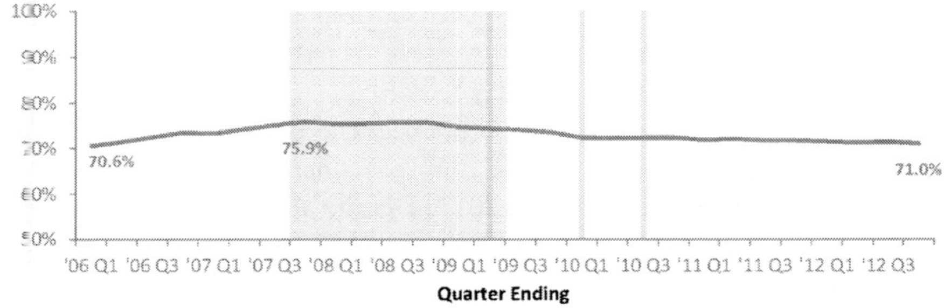

Source: CFPB Consumer Credit Panel; note: Y-axis does not start at zero.

Figure 28. % of Consumers Age 18 and Older with Open General Purpose Credit Cards.

As we consider total credit line, it is worth addressing the distribution of accounts across individuals to determine whether the credit lines have become concentrated in a smaller part of the population. While the CCDB does not enable such a comparison because there is no information linking accounts to individuals, we can look at the percent of the adult population with a credit card in the CFPB Consumer Credit Panel.

The data show that the percentage of the adult population holding a credit card rose prior to the financial crisis, peaked at 75.9% at the end of 2007, and then gradually declined back to 2006 levels by the end of 2012. Approximately 71.0% of the population has at least one credit card trade line in 2012.

Total Small Business Credit Line

As previously discussed, the small business credit card market provides a useful, albeit inexact, point of comparison to look for evidence of specific CARD Act impacts. To establish a standardized comparison, we only included industry participants that issue credit cards to both consumers and small businesses. We find that total small business credit line also experienced a significant decline over the same period. By Q4 2010, small business card line and consumer card line had declined in parallel, with small business line dropping to 73.5% of where they were in Q2 2008 and consumer line dropping to 75.5%. Small business line increased slightly to 76.5% of Q2 2008 levels during this period of time, while consumer line continued to drop, reaching 73.5% of Q2 2008 levels by Q4 2012.

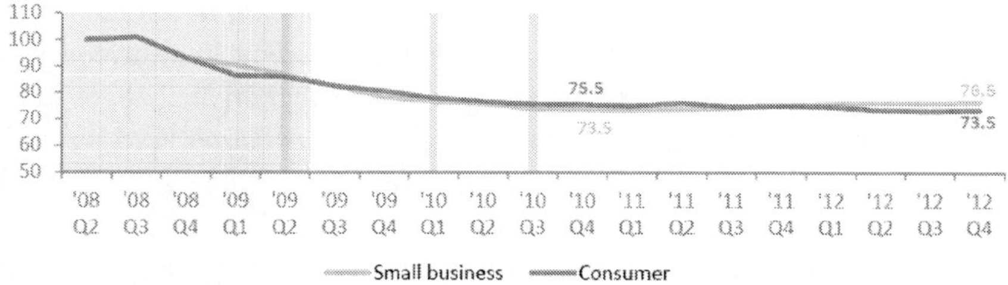

Source: CCDB; note: compares only issuers that participate in both product types; Y-axis does not start at zero.

Figure 29. Total Credit Line – Consumer vs. Small Business (Indexed tO 100 in Q2 2008).

The fact that consumer and small business lines closely tracked each other from 2008 to 2012 suggests that the Act – which, as we have noted, applies only to consumer cards and not small business cards – cannot explain the decline in consumer card line. Our analysis of the drivers of change in total credit line in the consumer card and small business card markets sheds some further light on this point.

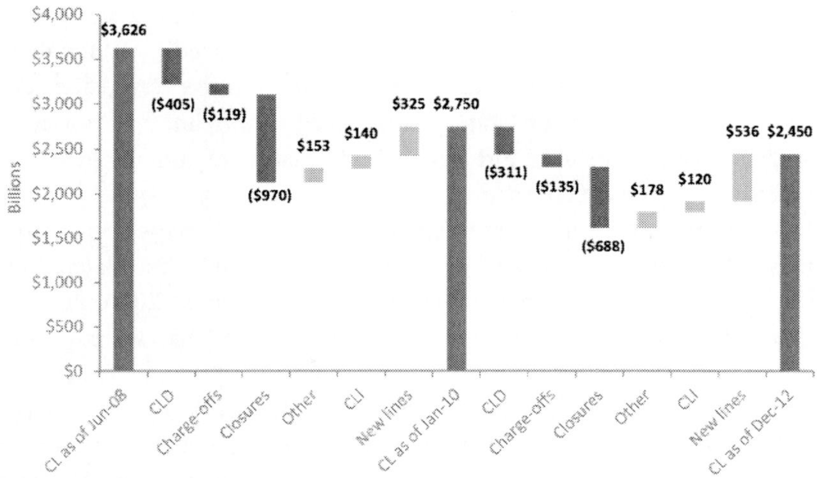

Source: CCDB*.

Figure 30. Drivers of Change in Total Credit Line.

* The Other category represents the net of portfolio acquisition and divestiture activity for the issuers included in the sample as well as the other factors that may change total available credit line.

3.3.2. Drivers of Change in Total Credit Line for Consumer Cards

In order to better understand the change in total credit line for consumer cards, using the CCDB data we looked at the actions that drive changes in line such as line extension practices, including credit line increase ("CLI") activity and new line origination, and line reduction practices, including line closures and credit line decrease ("CLD") activity.

The main driver of reductions to total line for consumer cards was account closures, as over 275 million accounts were closed from July 2008 to December 2012, driving a $1.7 trillion reduction in total line.* Approximately 60% of the account closures over the period of time from Q3 2008 to Q4 2012 were inactive accounts. At one point in 2009, about 17% of all inactive accounts were closed within the span of a single month. Closures were concentrated in 2008 and 2009, and some issuers announced that these closures were tied to risk management efforts related to the financial crisis. For example, in its 10-K filing for the fiscal year ended December 31, 2009, Bank of America disclosed a $274 billion reduction in unused credit line "driven primarily by account management initiatives on higher risk customers in higher risk states and inactive accounts."[56] In its 2009 Annual Report, JP Morgan Chase disclosed "further action to reduce risk associated with lending commitments" that included "certain inactive credit card lines [that] have been closed and a number of active lines [that] have been reduced."[57] While this did have the effect of reducing total credit line, and by extension credit availability, the impact on consumers was muted as this line had not been in use prior to account closure. More detailed information regarding closures will be discussed in a subsequent section.

Beyond account closures, credit line decreases and charge-offs contributed to lower total credit line in the market. Credit line decreases totaled $715.8 million, 57% of which occurred prior to February 2010, a major implementation date of the CARD Act. These lines, too, were generally unused.

These line reducing activities were partially offset by new account originations and credit line increase activity. The amount of credit line increase activity noticeably declined after the implementation of the CARD Act, particularly where a consumer did not request a line increase and thus did not supply current information on his/her income. Under these circumstances, part of the reason that issuers have been cautious about proactively

* For purposes of our analysis we excluded account closures that were preceded by a charge-off and show those line reductions in the charge-off category.

implementing credit line increases is that they have been uncertain about how to apply the CARD Act ability-to-pay requirements. As a result, the incidence of credit line increases has fallen dramatically as discussed in greater detail later in this report.

Closure Activity

Closing accounts represents one of the more aggressive approaches issuers take to adjust for risk exposure. As stated above, closure activity drove the bulk of the reductions in the time period before and after the implementation of the CARD Act. The overall spike in account closure rate in 2009 aligns with the financial crisis and is consistent with issuer comments mentioned earlier.

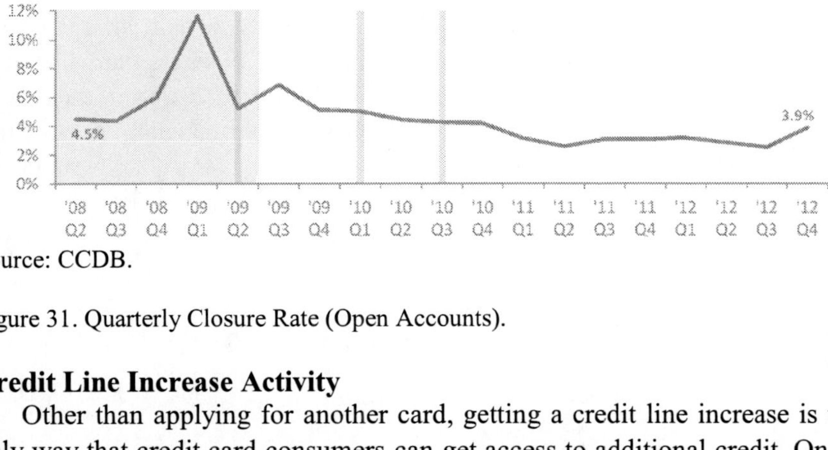

Source: CCDB.

Figure 31. Quarterly Closure Rate (Open Accounts).

Credit Line Increase Activity

Other than applying for another card, getting a credit line increase is the only way that credit card consumers can get access to additional credit. On an aggregate level, the incidence rate of CLI has dropped significantly since 2008.

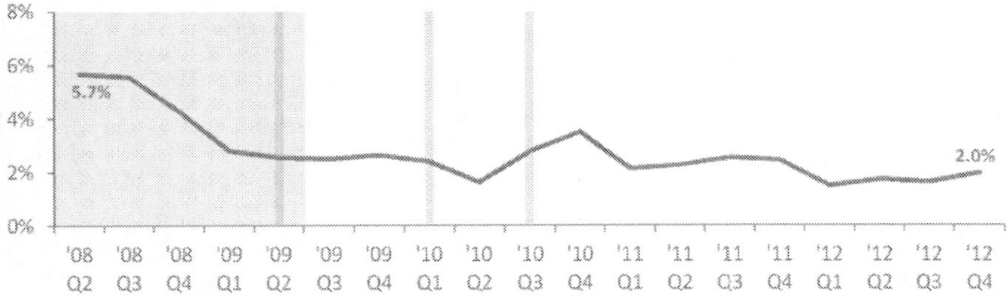

Source: CCDB.

Figure 32. Quarterly Incidence Rate of CLI (Open Accounts).

The incidence rate of CLI fell significantly after the financial crisis, bottoming out in Q2 of 2010. Since then the incidence rate of CLI has increased but is still 34.7% of its Q2 2008 level. The ability-to-pay requirement may play a role in fewer incidents of credit line increases as issuers are now required to include some consideration of the consumer's income in evaluating the consumer's ability to pay. The CFPB is actively engaged in understanding the impact on consumers of the reduced incidence rate of CLI.

3.3.3. Drivers of Change in Total Credit Line for Small Business Cards

As noted, the change in total line for small business credit cards can be used as a comparison for consumer cards. We have seen that the overall downward trend is consistent with business credit cards, and, as the figure below shows, the contributing factors are largely consistent as well. The charts below disaggregates changes in consumer and small business card lines for two time periods, first from June 2008 through January, 2010 and then from January, 2010 through the end of 2012 for issuers participating in both the consumer and small business markets.

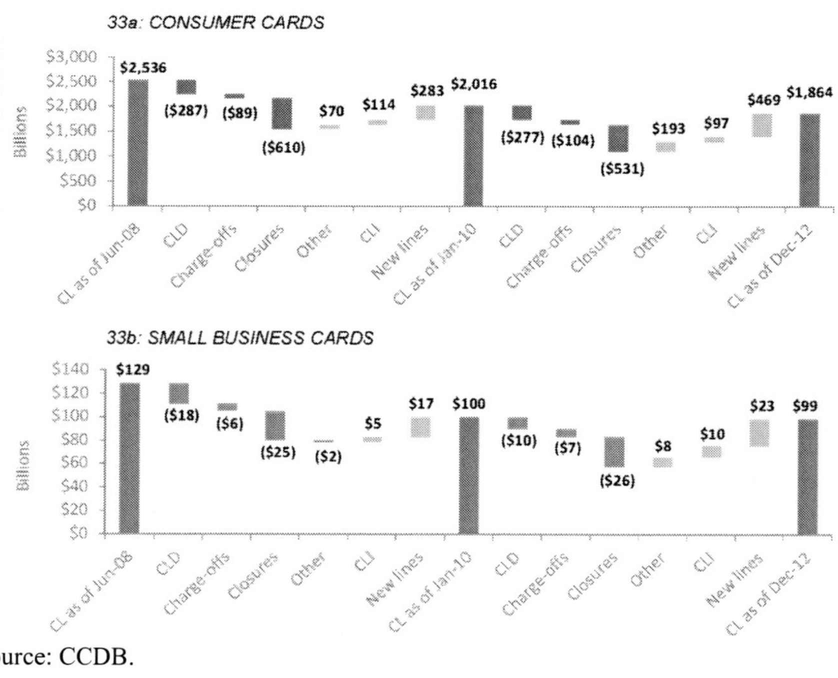

Source: CCDB.

Figure 33. Drivers of Change in Total Credit Line.

Small business card line experienced a net decrease in the total credit line of only 1.5% compared to 7.5% for consumer cards from January 2010 through December 2012. The factor that differentiates the two markets appears to be credit line increases. For consumer accounts, CLIs generated a 4.8% increase in total credit line; for small business cards, CLIs generated a 10.2% increase. Indeed, a comparison of the rate of credit line increases shows a directional divergence in the late 2011 time frame that persists through 2012. Other factors appear to be consistent between the two products.

From January 2010 through December 2012, line decreases, charge-offs, and closures resulted in a 43.0% reduction in credit line for small business cards; for consumer cards the comparable figure was 45.2%. New accounts generated a 22.6% increase in line for small business cards; for consumer cards the figure was 23.3%.

3.4. Conclusion

Across most of the metrics we have examined, credit availability appears to have tightened during 2008 and 2009 and to have loosened in the following years. Nonetheless, across all of these metrics, credit appears to be less available today than it was in 2007. This is especially true in the subprime market. Even so, it is important to note that total unused credit line for consumers in the credit card marketplace is $1.9 trillion and even in the subprime market there is $38.6 billion in unused credit card line.

That credit is less available today than it was in 2007 is hardly surprising. Credit is known to be cyclical. The Great Recession resulted in substantial credit losses not only in the mortgage market but in other credit markets as well including, of course, the consumer credit card market. When creditors experience large increases in credit losses, they may be inclined to implement more restrictive credit standards which disproportionately impact those with lower credit scores.

Except as noted below, nothing in the evidence reviewed suggests that the CARD Act was responsible for the reduction in credit access – which largely preceded the Act's enactment – or that the CARD Act has retarded the pace of the recovery. The parallels between the consumer credit card market and the small business credit card market, and between the credit card market and other consumer credit markets, do not suggest that, in general, recovery in the card marketplace has been negatively impacted by the CARD Act.

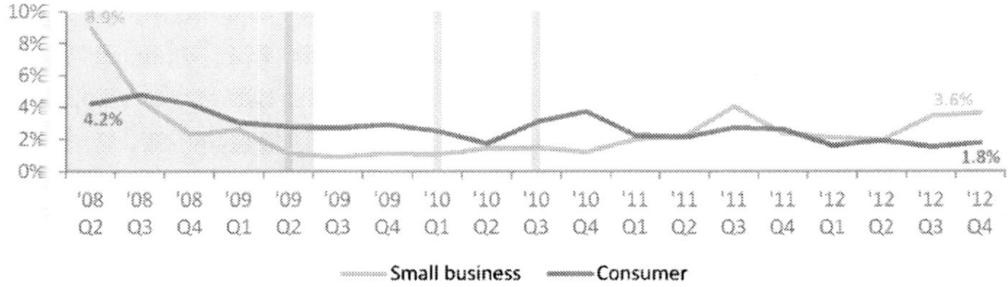

Source: CCDB.

Figure 34. Quarterly Incidence Rate of CLI – Consumer vs. Small Business (Open Accounts).

There are a few areas in which the CARD Act has, by design, restricted access to credit. This is true for students and young people and for consumers whose income and assets do not reflect an ability to pay a new extension of credit when opening a new credit card account or increasing the line on an existing account. This may explain why the incidence of credit line increases has likewise lagged in the consumer card space.

Because accounts with superprime credit scores generally have plenty of unused line available and deep subprime lines are associated with the greatest risk, prime and core subprime would be the most likely segments to experience proactive CLIs. The Bureau plans to study how limitations on proactive line increases are impacting these segments of consumers.

4. Agreements, Disclosures, and Issuer Practices

4.1. Introduction

The purpose of this section is to look at changes in credit card agreements, the practices of credit card issuers, and the effectiveness of disclosures as set forth in the CARD Act. These are broad topics, and each could easily warrant longer treatments. However, for purposes of this round of the report, we narrowed the focus to a few areas. The review of agreements focuses on the presentation of terms and the readability of the documents. The disclosure review effort centers on the periodic statement disclosure and the minimum payment warning required by Title II of the CARD Act. [58] In terms of issuer practices, we look at risk-based pricing in light of the CARD Act's limitations on APR changes and we look at interest rate reviews – a new requirement introduced in the CARD Act.

4.2. Terms and Conditions of Agreements

Prior to the CARD Act, credit card issuers generally reserved the right to change the interest rate on credit card accounts and balances at their discretion. Issuers also typically applied customer payments to the balance with the lowest interest rate first which preserved higher cost debt and increased the interest earned by issuers. All of these actions were spelled out in cardholder agreements prior to the CARD Act. This section examines changes in cardholder agreements since 2008 and following enactment of the CARD Act.

4.2.1. Changes to Cardholder Agreements

As part of the CCPI, the Bureau identified credit card products that were offered in both 2008 and 2012, and obtained complete copies of the accompanying cardholder agreements that were in place at both points in time. One product was identified for each of the participating issuers. These products were chosen in order to isolate the effects of agreement changes, rather than those deriving from inherent product differences. While the subsequent comparisons are drawn for a limited set of credit card products, the Bureau views these agreements as generally indicative of the practices of a set of issuers representing approximately 80% of credit card industry balances.

Cardholder Agreement Conformity to Card Act Requirements

Our review of this select set of cardholder agreements shows that, not surprisingly, post-Act issuers generally aligned their agreements with CARD Act requirements. Provisions for overlimit fees have become increasingly rare, and if present, are accompanied by clear indications that prior customer consent is required. Consistent with the safe harbor of the implementing rule, nearly every agreement studied provided for a penalty fee on late/returned payments of $25 or less for a first violation, and $35 or less for subsequent violations within six billing cycles. In addition, the language in each agreement has been modified to be consistent with the Act's requirement regarding payment allocation (i.e. the application of payments in excess of the minimum amount due to the highest APR balances).[59] Most cardholder agreements studied reserve the right to raise APRs on future balances subject to 45 days advance notice. The Bureau also observed that some issuers removed provisions for penalty APRs.*

Changes to Cardholder Agreement Length and Form

One of the expressed goals of the CARD Act was to improve transparency in the credit card market, but the Act did not explicitly mandate any changes in the length and form of credit card agreements. Under regulations adopted by the Board that were republished concurrently with the February 2010 CARD Act regulations, issuers were required in July 2010 to include along with the account opening agreement a "Schumer box" containing tabular disclosure of key terms.

Our analysis of the cardholder agreements shows that many issuers streamlined the presentation and content of their cardholder agreements between 2008 and 2012. For instance, during this period, many of these issuers were able to comply with additional disclosure rules set forth by Regulation Z, while also consolidating the terms and conditions of their cardholder agreements into fewer documents.[60] Despite this consolidation, post-CARD Act agreements studied by the Bureau are on average shorter than their corresponding pre-CARD Act versions.† Figure 35 below illustrates that the average word count of studied cardholder agreements fell 24.4% between 2008 and 2012. Indeed, every cardholder agreement for which the Bureau was able to assess agreement length displayed a decrease in length since 2008.

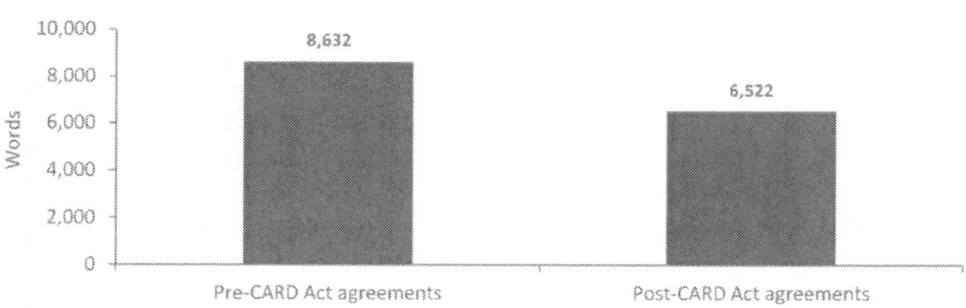

Source: CCPI and CFPB analysis.

Figure 35. Average Word Count.

* However, these agreements, as well as every other agreement reviewed by the Bureau, reserve the general right to change agreement terms (including APRs).

† For 2008, we relied upon agreements provided to us by issuers. These documents generally did not include the rate and fee disclosures that are now presented on issuer websites as part of the account agreement. Given that such rate and fee information presumably was incorporated by reference into the 2008 agreements, Figure 35 likely understates the true discrepancy in agreement length between 2008 and 2013.

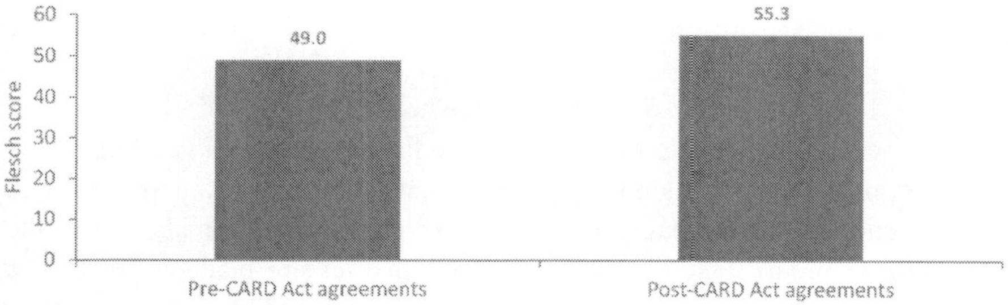

Source: CCPI and CFPB analysis.

Figure 36. Average Flesch Readability Score (Higher Numbers Indicate Greater Readability).

Moreover, cardholder agreements have generally improved in terms of readability and accessibility since 2008. As indicated below in Figure 36, most of the agreements studied by the Bureau are more readable today than in 2008 according to the Flesch readability score, a widely used standard in plain language analysis.

The Bureau's review also indicated that today's cardholder agreements employ fewer terms-of- art than agreements prior to the passage of the CARD Act. Nearly every agreement we studied has replaced industry jargon such as "finance charge" with more straightforward language such as "interest charge." The Bureau's analysis of cardholder agreements using the Flesch-Kincaid grade level metric is consistent with this observation. As shown in Figure 37 below, the average Flesch-Kincaid grade level associated with today's agreements is lower than the average grade level associated with their pre-CARD Act precursors – suggesting that today's agreements are more accessible than older agreements.

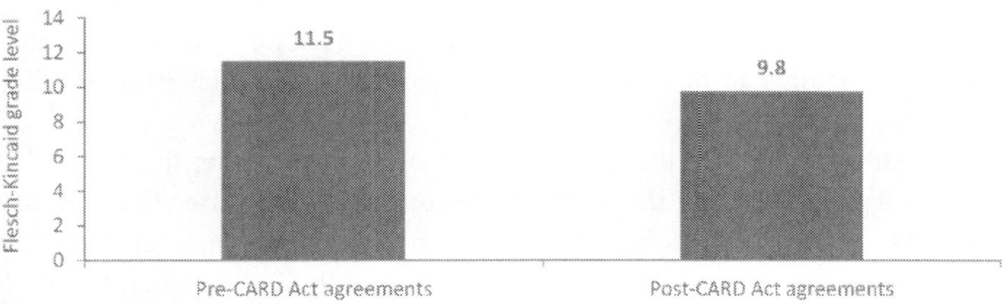

Source. CCPI and CFPB analysis.

Figure 37. Average Flesch-Kincaid Grade Level (Lower Numbers Indicate Greater Readability).

4.3. Periodic Statement Disclosures

Title II of the CARD Act, entitled "Enhanced Consumer Disclosures," sets out new disclosure requirements for periodic statements, including (1) a minimum payment warning on billing statements showing the amount that will be paid and the repayment period length if the consumer makes only the minimum payment[61] assuming no additional charges are made, as well as a comparison to a three-year payoff schedule, and (2) disclosure on billing statements of the due date and, if different, the date on which a late penalty will be charged together with the amount of any fee or penalty rate associated with late payments.[62]

At their core, disclosures are intended to affect consumer behavior by making the consequences of particular choices more salient than they might otherwise be. For example, the CARD Act requirement that monthly statements feature a prominent disclosure on the consequences of making a late payment was most likely designed to affect the incidence of such payments by making the resulting costs of paying late more noticeable to consumers. Similarly, the disclosure requirement with respect to the consequence of making only minimum payments presumably was designed to affect the incidence of minimum payments by making their costs more salient. As such, the effectiveness of any disclosure hinges first on its ability to affect consumer awareness and comprehension of the information being disclosed.

Minimum Payment Warning

The CARD Act and its implementing regulations require issuers to include repayment disclosures on periodic billing statements.[63] The disclosures were designed to inform consumers of the monetary cost and time it will take to pay off a credit card balance if they only make the minimum monthly payment.

Figure 38 showcases the minimum payment warning developed by the Board and required to be included in periodic statements after February 22, 2010.[64]

As part of the CCPI, the Bureau sought information about the minimum payment warning box and its placement in consumer disclosures. Each issuer respondent reported providing the minimum payment warning in both the paper and electronic (downloadable PDF) versions of billing statements.

The Bureau further asked issuers about the effect that these disclosure requirements have had on credit card payments, particularly among those consumers previously paying only the minimum amount. A small minority of respondents reported comparing the payment behavior on accounts several cycles before and after the disclosure changes, and found a reduction in the percentage of consumers making only the minimum payment.* Initial findings in this area suggest that this represents another area for possible additional research by the Bureau.

Beyond the impact on repayments, the Bureau asked if issuers track either (1) the percentage of consumers receiving an electronic billing statement, or (2) the percentage of consumers opening that statement prior to making an online payment. Less than half of respondents actively track such behaviors. The issuers that do found that an average of 38% of consumers made at least one payment online and, separately, that an average of 25% of consumers made all payments exclusively online or through automatic payment. Most issuers report being able to track the percentage of consumers opening an electronic bill prior to making an online payment, and they report that on average 26% of consumers access their electronic bill before making an online payment. It is worth noting that this figure does not capture consumers who may review a paper billing statement prior to making an online payment.

Minimum Payment Warning: If you make only the minimum payment each period, you will pay more in interest and it will take you longer to pay off your balance. For example:		
If you make no additional charges using this card and each month you pay	You will pay off the balance shown on this statement in about	And you will end up paying an estimated total of
Only The Minimum Payment	10 Years	$3,284
$62	3 Years	$2,232 *(Savings = $1,052)*
If you would like information about credit counseling services, call 1-800-xxx-xxxx.		

Source: Board Model Notice.

Figure 38. Minimum Payment Warning.

* Claudine Gartenberg's research presented at a 2011 CARD Act conference sponsored by the CFPB (*"The Impact of the CARD Act on Cardholder Repayment Rates"*) showed that the minimum payment disclosure led to an overall decline in the number of minimum payments by "reframing" the payment decision for consumers. Counterintuitively, this research also seemed to suggest that customers shifting to the 36-month payment reduced debt more slowly than did those not shifting to the higher repayment figure. One possible reason might be that consumers shift away from lump-sum payment behavior when paying more than the minimum. This analysis was done on a small sample of credit union accounts, and the findings suggest there is significant potential learning in the area of consumer payment decisions.

All respondents offer online payment options and electronic billing statements. However, none provide the minimum payment warning on the payment screen in their online account portal, and very few issuers show the minimum payment warning on screens leading up to an online payment transaction. For the vast majority of respondents' online portals, a consumer can see the information disclosed in the minimum payment warning (including the three year repayment disclosure) only by opening the electronic billing statement or viewing a paper statement as this is where the disclosure is currently required to appear.

As such, these results suggest that a meaningful number of consumers may not see the minimum payment warning due to the use of an online payment portal, where disclosures are not required and are generally not present. To the extent this is true, there is no opportunity for the disclosures to affect the consumer's understanding or the consumer's behavior.

4.4. Issuer Practices

4.4.1. Risk-Based Pricing

Risk-based pricing is the practice by lenders of offering different consumers different interest rates or other loan terms, based on the estimated risk that a customer will fail to pay back the loan. Under risk-based pricing, for the same credit card an issuer may offer a lower interest rate to customers viewed as lower risk based on a number of factors that may include having a higher credit score. Thus, for example, for any given product consumers with superprime scores generally receive a lower APR than consumers with subprime scores.

Prior to enactment of the CARD Act, the ability of issuers to reprice existing accounts and balances allowed issuers to "correct" pricing if their initial assessment of risk proved incorrect. At the same time, because issuers were free to reprice it was not necessary to set interest rates based upon the issuers' upfront assessment of risk. Consumer advocates and industry representatives disagreed as to the extent to which the repricing practices that prevailed prior to the Act were designed to tie pricing to risk. In the wake of CARD Act limitations on the ability to change interest rates after account origination (especially on existing balances), some issuers suggested that there would be a reduction in their ability to effectively price to risk as the initial pricing is necessarily harder to adjust.

Figure 39 below shows that risk-based pricing has persisted in the industry from 2008 to 2012. New accounts originated in the year continue to show that higher risk accounts (lower FICO scores) have much higher interest rates than lower risk accounts (higher FICO scores). In particular, the spread at origination between the lowest FICO score range and the highest widened from 240 basis points in 2008 to 440 basis points in 2012.

The difference between APRs on high risk vs. low risk accounts in both years shows that risk- based pricing is still a common practice in the credit card space. The widening of the difference suggests that the extent of risk-based pricing has actually *increased* since 2008.* This may mean that more of the costs associated with owning and using a credit card is reflected in the APR for accounts with subprime credit scores, and as a result the APR may have become a more useful indicator of what consumers can expect to pay to own and use a credit card.

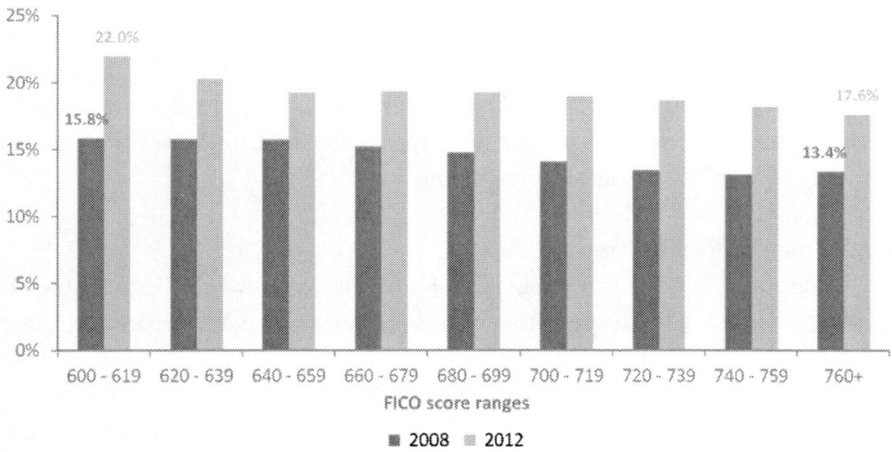

Source: CCDB.†

Figure 39. Retail APR for New General Purpose Accounts (Excludes Promotional Interest Rates).

* This is consistent with the idea, suggested by Oren Bar-Gill and Ryan Bubb, that restrictions on back-end pricing will result in greater use of ex-ante (upfront) risk-based pricing because prices changes based on ex-post observations of risk are less feasible. *See* Oren Bar-Gill & Ryan Bubb, *Credit Card Pricing: The CARD Act and Beyond*, 97 Cornell L. Rev. 967, 969 (2012).

† New accounts booked with an initial APR of 3.99% or less were deemed to be in receipt of a promotional interest rate and these accounts were excluded from the calculation

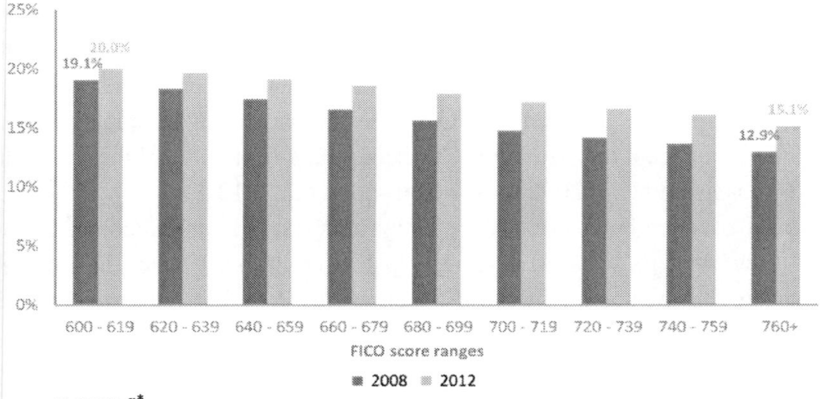

Source: CCDB.[x*]

Figure 40. Retail APR for Mature General Purpose Accounts (Open Accounts, Excludes Promotional Interest Rates and New Accounts).

In contrast to the new accounts, existing accounts show a smaller margin between the lowest and the highest FICO scores in 2012 (490 bps) than that in 2008 (620 bps). The narrowing of the difference indicates a decline in risk-based pricing on existing accounts, perhaps attributable to the restrictions on repricing by card issuers as required by the Act.

4.4.2. Interest Rate Reviews

Under the CARD Act, whenever an issuer increases the interest rate on an account – either with respect to existing balances or with respect to new transactions – the issuer generally is required to review the account at least once every six months to determine whether the factors underlying the increase have changed and to reduce the interest rate where indicated by the review.[65] This rule applies to interest rate increases that occurred any time after January 1, 2009.[66]

As part of the CCPI, we requested information on interest rate increases from January 1, 2009, as indicated in the CARD Act, to February 21, 2010, immediately prior to one of the major implementation dates of the CARD Act. The responding banks reported raising interest rates on 154.3 million credit card accounts prior to the CARD Act, and the balances associated with these accounts totaled $184.6 billion at the time of repricing. These accounts are subject to the rate review every six months as described above.

* Accounts with an APR of 3.99% or less were deemed to be in receipt of a promotional interest rate and these accounts were excluded from the calculation.

As of December 2012, 15.2 million or 9.9% of these accounts received a full interest rate reduction back to the original APR. An additional 21.8 million accounts, or 14.1% of these accounts, received a reduction but not to the original APR. As illustrated in Figure 41 below, the remaining 117.3 million accounts remain at the higher interest rate, though issuers are still required to evaluate these accounts for rate reductions every six months so these rates may be lowered in the future.

For accounts reduced to the original APR after the required six month reviews, interest rates were reduced by an average of 5.0 percentage points. For accounts that received a partial reduction, the average APR decline was 2.8 percentage points. If consumers who received these rate reductions kept their balances constant for one year following the rate reduction, this provision of the CARD Act would reduce consumer interest payments by approximately $2.1 billion among the issuers participated in the CCPI. While, we do not have specific information about these accounts to validate an assumption that balances remained unchanged for one year, we view this calculation as a relatively conservative estimate of the savings to consumers since we limited the analysis only to accounts receiving an interest rate increase between January 1, 2009 and February 21, 2010. Another 13.9 million accounts received interest rate increases between February 22, 2010 and December 31, 2012, and 3.8 million of those accounts subsequently received interest rate reductions.

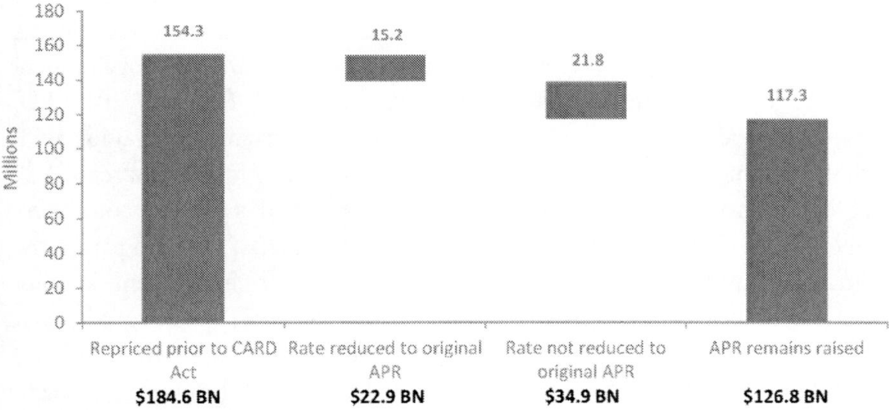

Source: CCPI.

Figure 41. Accounts Experiencing an Interest Rate Increase between Jan. 1, 2009 and Feb. 22, 2010 ($ Figures Represent Outstanding Balances Associated with These Accounts).

While the review provision has resulted in interest rate reductions for millions of cardholders, the reduction is a rollback of interest rate increases that may have been undertaken, at least in part, in response to (or in anticipation of) the CARD Act.

5. Product Innovation

The CARD Act calls upon the Bureau to assess whether and to what extent implementation of the Act has affected "innovation." This is inherently a complex task, and the most the Bureau can plausibly do is to scan the credit card marketplace for evidence of post-CARD Act innovation.

In the post-CARD Act marketplace, there are some innovative product structures that aim to be consumer friendly. One example is a program that allows customers to develop customizable payment plans based on self-defined preferences. Using an interactive dashboard, consumers can select individual purchases, perform "what-if" scenarios with chosen payment amounts or frequencies, and ultimately commit to specific repayment options. In addition, the program also provides customers with other novel disclosures and opportunities to monitor spending and track progress towards meeting general financial goals.

Credit card issuers have also adopted social media and other technology platforms not just for marketing purposes, but also as an active tool for customer service and accountholder engagement. Several market participants have updated their support operations, and even certain product development activities, to incorporate feedback from social media. A February 2013 J.D. Power & Associates survey found that 71% of all consumers engaging with credit card companies through social media outlets did so for service reasons.[67] A recent Board study found that roughly one third of surveyed consumers received some form of "payment due" text message alerts.[68] Moving from the realm of account management to prospective consumer engagement, another issuer announced a program in 2012 that uses interactive features of social media to "crowd source" desired terms for its consumer credit card offerings, including such items as interest rates, fees, and call center locations. As such, issuers continue to take advantage of new technological trends in bringing to market new products and accompanying services.

The Bureau readily acknowledges that the imposition of new substantive rules in the CARD Act, was intended, by design, to preclude certain forms of innovation deemed harmful to consumers (e.g. experimentation with new forms of back-end pricing). Similarly, to the extent innovation depends on sources of revenue other than upfront fees and front-end APRs, the Act may well be inhibiting such novelties.

To the extent that the CARD Act created basic standards and a more level playing field, and thus a base for consumer-friendly innovation, it is perhaps no coincidence that some of the new products that have emerged in the past two years have focused on delivering simple and transparent account features and terms.

Indeed, several independent surveys and reports have reported all-time highs for both consumer satisfaction and assessed transparency, and have even gone so far as to directly attribute such changes to the CARD Act.[69] J.D. Power released its 2013 U.S. Credit Card Satisfaction Study which showed credit card satisfaction at an all-time high since the inception of the study in 2007. It showed that "overall, customers appear to be increasingly happy with their credit cards" and a J.D. Power spokesperson attributed part of the increase to "recent changes in the credit card industry, such as the Credit Card Accountability Responsibility and Disclosure Act of 2009, [that] had a positive impact on consumers."[70] Despite the fact that consumers may not completely understand the terms and benefits on their cards,[*] the industry experienced improved satisfaction scores for the fourth consecutive year.[71]

6. Adequacy of Protections

The CARD Act made sweeping changes in the credit card marketplace and addressed many of the practices that consumer advocates had identified as particularly problematic. Voluntary actions taken by card issuers have brought further improvements to the market. Additionally, the Bureau is continuing to work with card issuers on voluntary efforts to further shorten and simplify their cardholder agreements.

In this report, we highlight six examples of areas of concern in the credit card marketplace – practices that may pose risk to consumers and that will warrant further scrutiny by the Bureau.

* According to the J.D. Power 2013 U.S. Credit Card Satisfaction Study, less than 47% of consumers report that they completely understand their credit card terms, an increase from 32% in 2010.

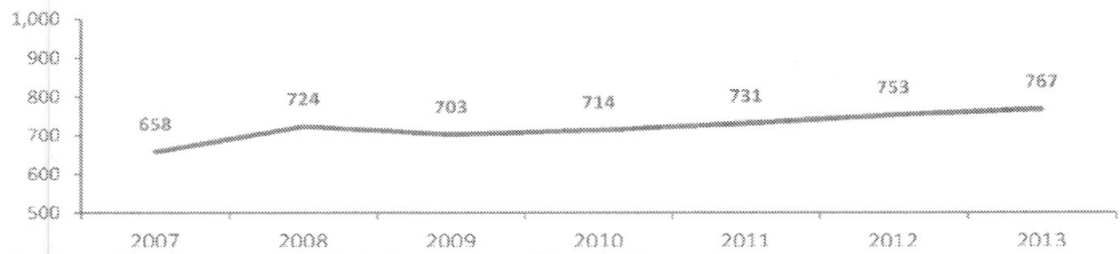

Source: J.D. Power and Associates; note: Y-axis does not start at zero.

Figure 42. J.D. Power Credit Card Satisfaction Index (based on a 1,000 Point Scale).

6.1. Add-on Products

Some credit card issuers market various "add-on" products to card users, including debt protection, identity theft protection, credit score monitoring, and other products that are supplementary to actual extension of credit. In September 2010, the Board proposed amendments to Regulation Z to require enhanced disclosures with respect to the marketing of certain add-on products across all forms of credit.[72] That rulemaking proceeding transferred to the Bureau in July 2011. The Bureau's supervisory and enforcement functions also have continued to focus on issues concerning add-on products. The Bureau's experience indicates that some credit card issuers have employed, or permitted third-party marketers to employ, deceptive promotional practices when marketing such products, including the failure to adequately disclose important product terms and conditions. In addition, some consumers appear to have been enrolled in programs without their affirmative consent, while others may have been billed for services that were not performed or activated. Furthermore, consumer complaints received by the Bureau also suggest that consumers may have been misled by the marketing and sales practices associated with some credit card add-on products.

The Bureau has brought a number of enforcement actions addressed to practices such as these and is continuing investigations in other cases. Indeed, as a result of add-on product enforcement actions brought by the Bureau and its partners, companies have paid substantial fines and restitution to consumers.[73] The Bureau also has issued a Bulletin[74] setting forth its expectations with respect to the marketing of these add-on products. The Bureau will continue to closely review the sale of add-on products by card issuers and their service providers to determine whether additional consumer protections are warranted.

6.2. Fee Harvesting

As part of the CARD Act, Congress addressed products commonly referred to as "fee harvester" cards. These products, which were marketed to customers with deep subprime credit scores, offered relatively low credit lines and high fees which were billed to the account and effectively reduced the credit extended to the consumer. In 2008, the FTC brought a prominent enforcement action against an issuer of such a product in which consumers were charged $185 in fees against a $300 credit line.[75]

The CARD Act and implementing regulations issued by the Board addressed this issue by providing that an issuer may not require consumers to pay fees (other than penalty fees) during the first year in which an account is opened which exceed 25% of the total initial credit line.[76]

In April 2011, the Board revised the implementing regulation it had issued to expand the fee limitation to fees that consumers were required to pay *prior* to account opening.[77] The change was based on the Board's understanding that certain credit card issuers were "requiring consumers to pay application or processing fees prior to account opening that, when combined with other fees charged to the account after account opening, exceed 25 percent of the account's initial credit limit."[78]

In response to the Board's revised rule, a credit card issuer filed suit in the United States District Court for the District of South Dakota, alleging that the Board exceeded its authority by expanding the rule to apply to fees a consumer is required to pay prior to account opening. The District Court granted a motion for preliminary injunction on September 23, 2011.[79]

Following the court's decision, the Bureau issued a proposal to amend Regulation Z to conform to the court's decision.[80] Many members of the public opposed the proposed rule, arguing that the proposed amendment would reduce protections for vulnerable consumers.[81] Consumer advocates and the New York State Office of the Attorney General expressed similar views.[82] The Bureau nonetheless decided to finalize the rule it had proposed[83] in order to resolve any uncertainty created by the South Dakota litigation.[84]

The Bureau will continue to monitor the use of application fees in connection with account opening to determine if it should take action under its available authorities. The Bureau notes that prior to passage of the CARD Act, the Board, OTS, and NCUA all adopted restrictions on fee harvesting, using their authority under section 5(a) of the Federal Trade Commission Act to prohibit unfair or deceptive practices, though they were withdrawn in light of the CARD Act.[85] The Bureau further notes that when Congress subsequently passed the CARD Act's limits on fee harvesting, it was explicit that such limits not be construed "as authorizing any imposition or payment of advance fees otherwise prohibited by any provision of law."[86]

6.3. Deferred Interest Products

6.3.1. Product Description

Deferred interest is a form of promotional financing typically linked to private label credit cards that consumers can use for large purchases. These offers retroactively assess and charge interest if the balance is not paid in fully by a specific date. The interest rate on these cards is often substantially higher than the rate on standard general purpose credit cards. As a result, for consumers who have available credit on a general purpose credit card and who cannot repay the entire balance during the deferred interest period, deferred interest promotions can sometimes be more expensive than revolving the same balance on their existing card. Deferred interest financing has been the subject of regulatory and legislative activity. As it relates to payment allocation, the CARD Act requires that payments in excess of the minimum payment in the last two months of a deferred interest promotion be allocated entirely to the promotional balance, and that promotional rate terms for all credit cards, including private label cards, must last a minimum of a six months.[87] Although the CARD Act itself did not specifically address deferred interest products in other aspects, the Board rules that went into effect on February 22, 2010[88] imposed several additional disclosure and marketing restrictions related to deferred interest finance, including:

- The disclosure of the timeframe of the promotional period and post-promotional APR must be clear and conspicuous; [89]
- Issuers may use the phrase "'no interest" or similar term to describe the possible avoidance of interest obligations only if they offer an "'if paid in full" caveat in a clear and conspicuous manner preceding the disclosure of the deferred interest period;[90]
- The deferred payment balance and deferred interest on periodic statements should be disclosed separately during the deferred interest period, with each identified by a separate term, such as "deferred interest balance" and "contingent interest charge" or "deferred interest charge";[91]

- During the deferred interest program, the creditor must disclose the end of the deferred interest period (i.e., the due date by which the deferred interest balance must be paid in order to avoid the obligation to pay interest on that balance). This disclosure must appear on the front of each periodic statement issued during the deferred interest period, beginning with the first periodic statement issued during that period that reflects the deferred interest transaction. The disclosure must be substantially similar to Model Form G-18(H) (Deferred Interest Periodic Statement Clause) which states: "You must pay your promotional balance in full by [date] to avoid paying accrued interest charges";[92] and
- At the request of the customer, the issuer can apply payments to the deferred interest balance rather than to higher-priced balances notwithstanding the general CARD Act rule governing payment allocation.[93]

6.3.2. Market and Borrower Profile

The Credit Card Practices Inquiry conducted by the Bureau demonstrates that deferred interest promotions have been less available or less utilized by customers with prime and subprime credit scores, with 2011 volume 25% below 2007 volume. In 2011, customers with superprime credit scores financed almost $19 billion in deferred interest purchases, up 22% since 2007. The customers with superprime credit scores thus accounted for over 60% of total deferred interest financing in 2011, an increase from 47% in 2007.[*] Unlike general credit card balances, deferred interest financing balances remained relatively stable throughout the Great Recession.

6.3.3. Payoff Rate

The payoff rate, measured by the percentage of deferred interest plans in which the full balance is repaid prior to the end of the deferred interest period divided by the total number of deferred interest plans originated, varies quite significantly by FICO score range, as illustrated below.[†] Interestingly, for the prime and subprime segments, the overall payoff rate increased for the 2010 vintage of deferred interest financing compared to the prior three years. This change coincides with disclosure requirements that became effective in

[*] Only includes promotions that expired at the end of 2012.

[†] Calculated on the promotion basis not account basis. It is not uncommon that one account can enter multiple promotions at different time and payoff rate is based on payoff behaviors of each promotional balance.

February 2010, and this change in payoff rate suggests that those disclosures may have affected payment behavior among these consumers.

Nonetheless, the fact that even after the new disclosures took effect, only 56.9% of consumers with scores below 660 successfully paid off their balance at the end of the promotional period raises concern. The contrast with the higher-scoring group is striking.

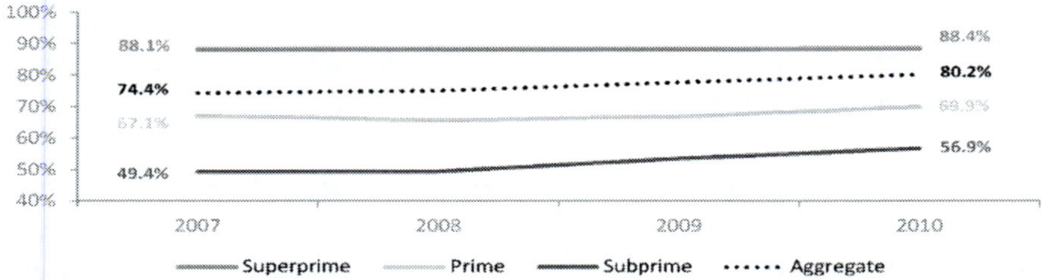

Source: CCPI; note: Y-axis does not start at zero.

Figure 43. Balance Payoff Rate for Deferred Interest Products.

6.3.4. Remaining Concerns

The evidence reviewed above highlights the potential risks to consumers posed by deferred interest products. In contrast to the promotional rates found in the general-purpose credit card market – which often provide an interest-free period with no potential retroactive assessment of interest – deferred interest products can end up costing a significant segment of vulnerable consumers a sizable amount of money. It is unclear whether those consumers appreciate the high interest rate risk that might occur at the end of the promotional period. It is also unclear what alternatives are available to these consumers or how they are impacted when they are retroactively assessed interest at a relatively high interest rate. At the same time, it is apparent that even among the subprime segment, a majority of consumers do obtain interest-free financing for a year. The Bureau intends to continue to study these issues and assess whether additional action is appropriate to promote a more fair and transparent market.

6.4. Transparency Issues

6.4.1. Disclosures on Online Payment Portals

Many of the regulations that the Bureau has inherited, including Regulation Z, were written primarily for a paper-and-pencil world. Applying these rules to a world in which communications are increasingly made electronically and transactions are undertaken electronically poses an important set of challenges.

As discussed in previous sections, minimum payment warnings provide one example of this general concern. These warnings are currently only required to be included on paper and electronic billing statements. As a result of the shift towards online methods of payment, an increasing number of consumers may fail to see any minimum payment disclosure in online account portals – thus defeating the point of the rule. At the same time, it is unclear how easily the full set of required disclosures, including the minimum payment warning and calculation and the three-year payoff calculation, could be translated into an online payment screen. The Bureau will observe closely how card issuers ensure that consumers receive disclosures in different channels.

6.4.2. Rewards

A 2011 Mercator Customer Monitor Survey showed that consumers said rewards were the number one reason to apply for a selected card.[94]

Further, Mercator's 2012 survey showed that "more credit and charge card owners (36%) said they try to use the credit card with the richest rewards than said they try to use the card with the lowest rates and fees (26%) or for purchases they want to finance (12%)."[96] As issuers compete more fiercely for high-spend transactors (i.e. consumers with high spending who do not carry an ongoing balance), certain issues and practices relating to rewards offerings and other marketing promotions may become a new area of concern.

- Frequently, rewards cards are marketed with an offer presented as a bonus for new cardholders. These bonuses may be presented as a certain number of "points" that will be awarded to the new cardholder, and sometimes those points are assigned a monetary value. The specific actions required to earn these bonuses may not always be presented clearly.
- Rewards are usually earned based on spending behavior with points accumulating in a cardholder's account, where they can ultimately be applied towards such benefits as free hotel accommodations, airline tickets, or cash. A rewards card might employ a variety of different formulas, some of which may evolve over time, require an explicit consumer opt-in on a frequent basis, or change according to purchase

type. Such complicated formulas may not always be disclosed in clear terms.

- Additionally, the value of rewards points and the rules governing rewards redemptions can be complex and difficult for consumers to understand and compare, especially at the application stage. There are usually certain "minimums" that must be earned before benefits can be accessed. The value of a "point" may vary based upon the number of points being redeemed or the product or service for which the points are being redeemed. In some instances the nominal value of a particular benefit may increase over time, progressively requiring more rewards points to access the same benefit

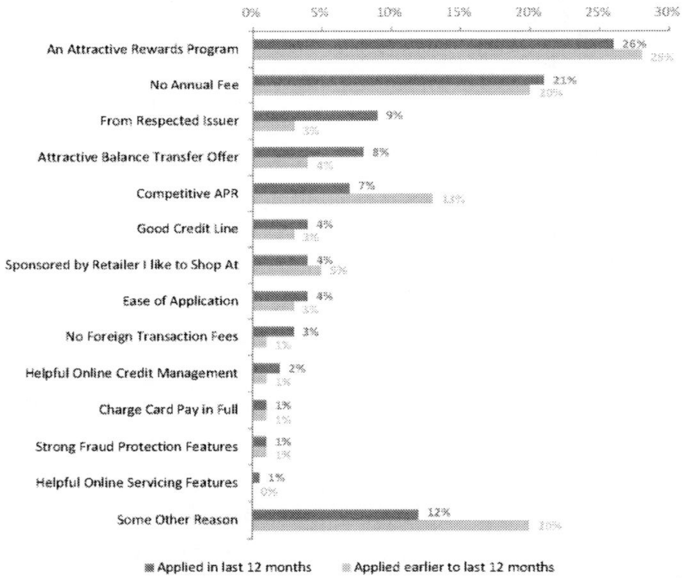

Source: Mercator Advisory Services Group 2011 Customer Monitor Survey.[95]

Figure 44. Consumers' Main Reason for Selecting Credit Card at Last Application (Base: Own Credit or Charge Card).

- The rewards picture is further complicated by the mechanisms used by issuers to assess points forfeiture and determine the cost of reinstating points from other sources. In some instances, customers may forfeit all unused points upon account closure, and there is wide variation in the conditions that may lead to points forfeiture in a given time period.

In its 2013 U.S. Credit Card Satisfaction Study,[97] J.D. Power found that consumer awareness of earning and redeeming rewards with their credit card has declined year over year, with 59% of customers saying they "completely" understand how to earn rewards in 2013, compared to 66% in 2012.[98] Furthermore, 33% of customers indicate they are unaware of the benefits associated with using their card.[99] In the course of its consumer research and market monitoring activities, the Bureau will review whether rewards disclosures are being made in a clear and transparent manner, as well as assess whether additional action is warranted.

6.4.3. Transparency of Grace Period

Most cards allow consumers to avoid paying interest on purchases when they pay their balance in full each month. This period between the end of a billing cycle and the payment due date is referred to as the “grace period.” This concept becomes more complicated when consumers fail to pay in full by the payment due date, as the grace period ceases to apply. When a grace period ceases to apply, interest is assessed on the unpaid balance from the beginning of the billing cycle and on new purchases made in the billing cycle and future billing cycles from the moment of a purchase until the consumer qualifies for the grace period again. It is worth noting that cash advances and balance transfers are generally not subject to a grace period and accrue interest from the transaction date. Regaining a grace period is another source of complexity as “trailing interest” comes into play. Trailing interest occurs when customers are assessed interest between the beginning of the billing cycle and the date on which they make payment in full. For consumers who pay their credit card balance in full each month, the grace period is a very simple concept to understand: they simply need to know when they must make payment to avoid an assessment of interest. But for consumers who revolve their balance, it is uncertain whether they understand that – unlike transactors -- they will be assessed interest on the unpaid balance from the beginning of the billing cycle and on new purchases made in the billing cycle and future billing cycles from the moment of a purchase until the consumer qualifies for the grace period again. And for consumers seeking to pay off their balance, it is unclear if they understand the potential for trailing interest. Disclosing these complexities in a clear manner is quite challenging. As with rewards products, the Bureau will review whether grace period limitations are being disclosed in a clear and transparent manner.

APPENDIX A: CARD ACT TIMELINE

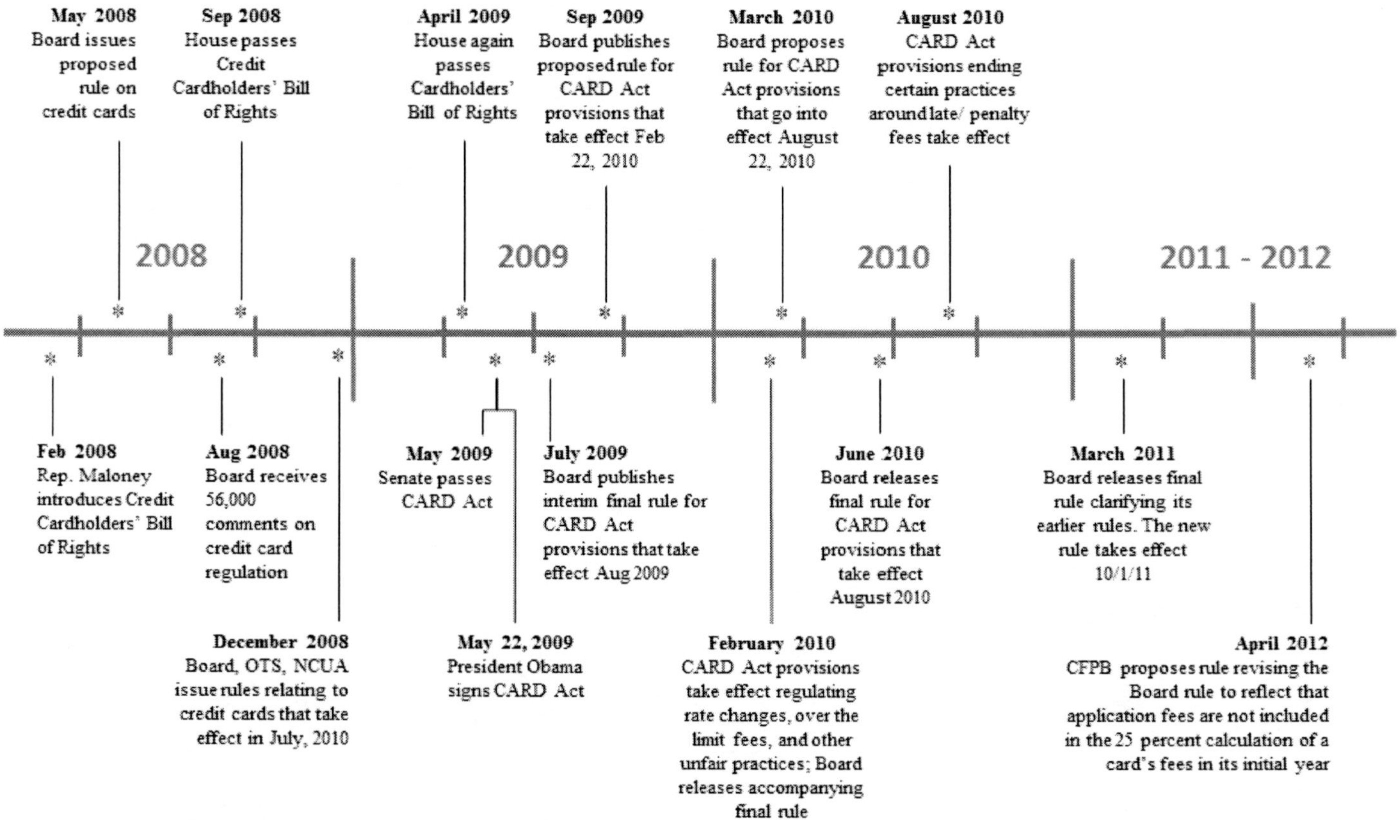

APPENDIX B: BREAKDOWN OF OTHER FEES

Total other fees declined from 2008 to 2012 and shown in Section 2 of this report. Some categories of other fees are addressed below. The source of all of this information is the CCDB.

Debt suspension and debt cancellation products are frequently marketed to credit cardholders as an add-on product. Consumers enrolled in the product generally are charged a fee each month which varies with the size of the month-end balance.

The quarterly incidence rate of debt suspension fees has experienced a relatively steady decline from 2008 to 2012, falling from 18.7% in Q2 2008 to 14.1% in Q4 2012. Accounts with core and deep subprime credit scores paying debt suspension fees fell from about 18% in Q4 2008 to about 12% in Q4 2012, while superprime, in contrast, showed a small enrollment change to 4.6% in Q4 2012 from 5.2% in Q4 2008. The incidence rate experienced the largest decline in 2012, falling 250 basis points from Q4 2011 to Q4 2012. This decline may be in part attributable to CFPB enforcement activity in this area.

The quarterly dollar volume of debt suspension fees has declined significantly from $773.8 million Q4 2008, to $458.3 million in Q4 2012. The decline is driven by a reduction in the total number of accounts, the incidence rate of accounts paying debt suspension fees, especially among customers with subprime credit scores, and potentially the average balance per enrolled account. The most significant decline in the volume of debt suspension fees occurred in 2009, and this may be a result of a reduction in accounts due to the recessionary macroeconomic events occurring at that time.

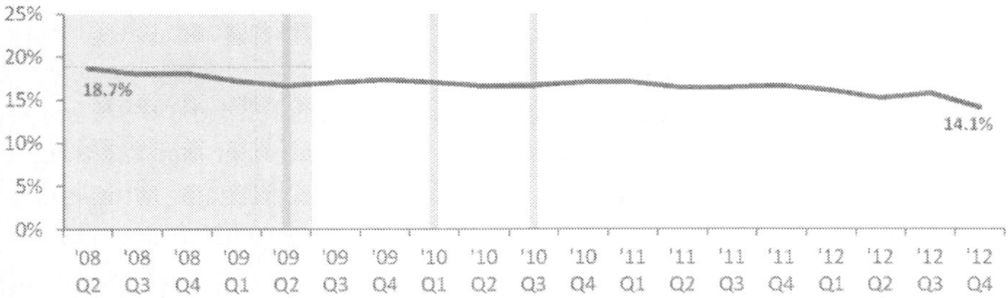

Source: CCDB; number of accounts paying debt suspension fees divided by number of active accounts.

Figure 45. Quarterly Incidence Rate of Debt Suspension Fees (Active Accounts).

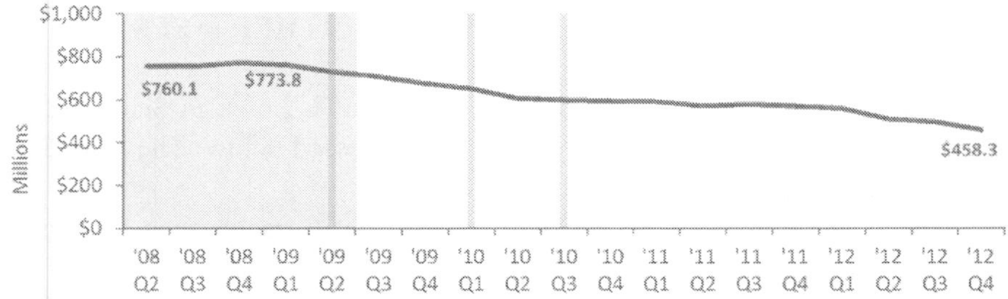

Source: CCDB.

Figure 46. Total Debt Suspension Fees.

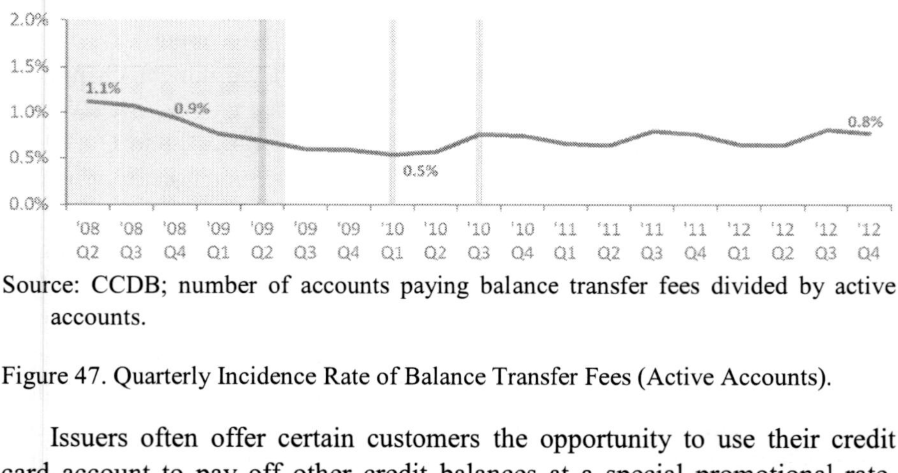

Source: CCDB; number of accounts paying balance transfer fees divided by active accounts.

Figure 47. Quarterly Incidence Rate of Balance Transfer Fees (Active Accounts).

Issuers often offer certain customers the opportunity to use their credit card account to pay off other credit balances at a special promotional rate. Consumers who receive such an offer and elect to avail themselves of it are generally charged a fee, calculated as a percentage of the amount transferred, sometimes with a floor and/or a ceiling. In some instances, issuers will offer to waive the fee, especially for new accounts.

The quarterly incidence rate of balance transfer fees fell from 0.9% in Q4 2008 to 0.8% in Q4 2012. However, the rate in 2012 is higher than the trough value of 0.5% in Q1 2010. Balance transfers may correspond with issuer appetite for debt, and the Q1 2010 low may indicate a reduced appetite for debt transfers due to the recession. Total volume of balance transfers dropped from $33.6 billion in Q4 2008 to $14.1 billion in Q4 2009, and has remained roughly at that level from 2010 through 2012.

Source: CCDB.

Figure 48. Total Balance Transfer Fees.

The total dollar volume of balance transfer fees also declined from Q4 2008 to Q1 2010, corresponding with the drop in total accounts and balance transfer incidence. However, since early 2010, issuers raised the balance transfer fee rate. As shown below, the balance transfer fee rose from 1.3% of balance transfer in Q4 2008 to a peak of 2.7% in Q3 2010, before settling at 2.0% of balance transfer amount in 2012.

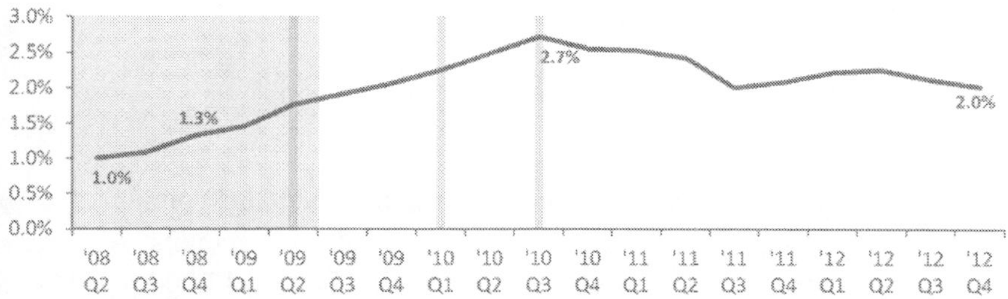

Source: CCDB; balance transfer fee as a % of balance transfer volume.

Figure 49. Cost of Balance Transfers.

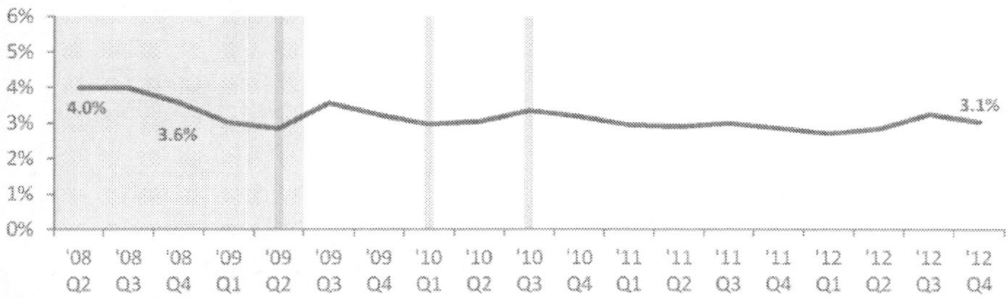

Source: CCDB; number of accounts paying a cash advance fee divided by number of active accounts.

Figure 50. Quarterly Incidence Rate of Cash Advance Fees (Active Accounts).

Consumers generally can use their credit cards to obtain cash at an ATM or from a bank teller. Issuers generally charge a fee when consumers do so, again stated as a percentage of the cash advance, often with a floor.

The quarterly incidence rate of cash advance fees fell modestly from 3.6% in Q4 2008 to 3.1% in Q4 2012. The decline in cash advance fees is a result of a decline in the number of accounts, a small decline in the incidence rate, an overall declining portfolio (the volume of cash advances fell from $9 billion in Q4 2008 to about $4 billion in Q4 2012), as well as a 30% reduction in size of cash advance per incident of cash advance.

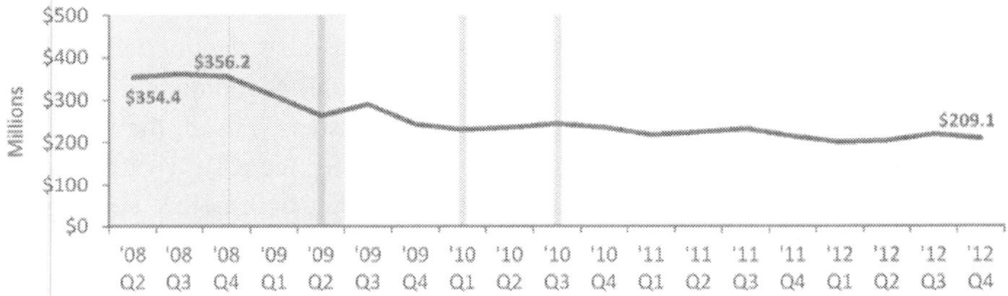

Source: CCDB.

Figure 51. Total Cash Advance Fees.

Total cash advance fees declined less rapidly than the volume of cash advances, as issuers raised the cash advance fee rate on accounts. As shown below, the fee cost of a cash advance rose from 3.9% in Q4 2008 to 4.9% in Q4 2012.

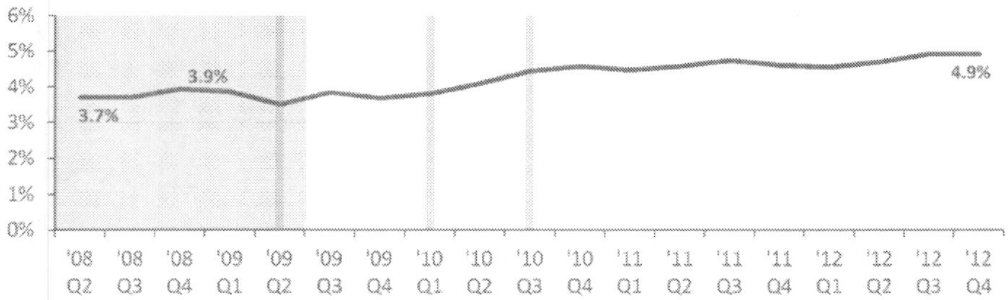

Source: CCDB; net cash advance fees divided by cash advance volume.

Figure 52. Cost of Cash Advances.

GLOSSARY

Defined Term

Ability to Pay: The rule covered in 12 CFR 1026.51(a), which states that a card issuer must not open a credit card account for a consumer or increase an account's credit limit unless the card issuer considers the consumer's ability to make the required minimum periodic payments under the terms of the account based on the consumer's income or assets and current obligations ("ability-to-pay rules").

Active Account: An account on which there has been any activity (e.g. any charge or any payment). In our CCDB, an active account is defined as an account on which there has been any activity during the preceding twelve months.

Approval Rate: The percentage of applicants that were approved for a credit card.

APR: The Annual Percentage Rate, which corresponds to the interest rate on an annualized basis.

APR (Introductory/ Promotional): The introductory or promotional APR that an issuer offers to a consumer, which after a set amount of time will convert or revert to the "retail APR" stipulated by the issuer. A promotional APR may apply only to purchases, only to balance transfers, or to both purchases and balance transfers.

Balance: The amount owed to a credit card issuer at any given point in time. This includes fees and interest.

Basis Point: 1/100 of a percentage point (i.e. 100 basis points is equivalent to 1 percentage point). For example, if an interest rate increases from 3.25% to 3.26%, it increased by 1 basis point. Abbreviated basis points.

Board: Federal Reserve Board of Governors

Bureau: Consumer Financial Protection Bureau ("CFPB" or "Bureau")

Card Act: Credit Card Accountability Responsibility and Disclosure Act of 2009

Cash Advance Fee: A fee charged when a consumer uses a credit card to receive cash such as by withdrawing cash from an ATM or writing a check drawn on the credit card account. This may be a flat fee or a percentage of the amount of the cash advance.

CCDB: "Credit Card Database," a database of information provided to the CFPB by credit card issuers that is managed by Argus Information and Advisory Services on the CFPB's behalf.

CCPI: "Credit Card Practices Inquiry," a source of supervisory information provided by selected issuers in responses to questions on issuer policies, procedures, and activities related to credit cards. The issuers participating in the CCPI represent approximately 80% of credit card balances.

Charge-Off: Refers to debt that creditors have deemed unlikely to be collected and that they have written off on their balance sheet. Charge-off does not relieve the consumer of their repayment requirement, and charged-off accounts are often pursued via collections processes.

Closure Rate: The number of accounts closed as a percentage of open accounts over a certain time period.

Consumer Card: Credit cards that are extended to consumers, which includes both general purpose and private label credit cards.

Core Subprime: The subset of FICO scores between 620 and 659; VantageScore 601-700 = D or Non-Prime.

Cost of Credit: The cost a consumer must pay to own and use a credit card.

Credit Balance: See "balance."

Credit Limit: The maximum amount of credit that a card issuer has agreed to extend to a consumer.

Credit Line: See "credit limit."

Credit Line Decrease ("CLD"): A practice whereby issuers reduce the credit limit associated with an account.

Credit Line Increase ("CLI"): A practice whereby issuers raise the maximum credit limit associated with an account. Credit line increases can be either proactive, where issuers voluntary raise consumer credit lines, or reactive, where consumers request a line increase, and issuers then determine whether or not to approve the request.

Cycle-Ending Balance: The balance on an account at the end of a billing period.

Deep Subprime: The subset of FICO scores that are below 620; VantageScore 501-600 = F or High Risk.

Deferred Interest Products: Arrangements that offer to delay (or defer) assessment of interest during a specified period of time and to assess interest only if the balance is not paid in full by the end of the specified period of time.

Delinquency: Failing to make a payment when due.

FDIC: Federal Deposit Insurance Corporation

Fee Harvesting: The practice of issuing credit cards to generate fee income via a variety of fees where the cardholder generally receives little credit to use for purchases in exchange for the fees paid.

Fee Yield: The dollar amount in fees assessed as a percentage of total balance.

FICO Score: A set of widely used risk scores developed by Fair Isaac Corporation ("FICO") to assess a consumer's creditworthiness. FICO scores range from 300 (low) to 850 (high), with lower scores indicating greater risk of default.

Flesch-Kincaid Readability Test: Readability tests designed to indicate the difficulty of comprehension.

FTC: Federal Trade Commission

General Purpose Credit Card: A credit card that is widely accepted by merchants that are not affiliates of the issuer for the purchase of products or services. These cards can generally be used wherever a particular network is accepted. Common networks are MasterCard, Visa, American Express and Discover.

Grace Period: The interval between the end of a billing cycle and the payment due date. No interest is assessed during this interval if a customer pays the balance in full before the payment due date and is not carrying a balance from month to month and has no cash advances outstanding.

Great Recession: The period of macroeconomic contraction occurring between December 2007 and June 2009, per the designation by the National Bureau of Economic Research.

Incidence Rate: The number of instances of an action in a given time period divided by the total accounts.

Interest Charge: The dollar amount charged by the issuer as interest for an incurred balance.

Late Fee: A charge levied against a cardholder when payments are not made by the due date.

Minimum Payment Warning: A disclosure that issuers are required to post on credit card statements that informs the consumer how long it will take to pay of the balance if the consumer only makes the minimum payment.

Non-Prime: See "Subprime."

Ncua: National Credit Union Administration

OCC: Office of the Comptroller of the Currency

Open-End Credit: Open-end credit means consumer credit extended by a creditor under a plan in which: (1) the creditor reasonably contemplates repeated transactions; (2) the creditor may impose a finance charge from time to time on an outstanding unpaid balance; and (3) the amount of credit that may be extended to the consumer during the term of the plan (up to any limit set by the creditor) is generally made available to the extent that any outstanding balance is repaid.

OTS: Office of Thrift Supervision

Outstandings: Typically refers to amounts owed to an issuer at an aggregate portfolio level at a given point in time. Used interchangeably with the term "balance."

Overlimit Fee: A fee charged when a consumer's total balance exceeds the amount stipulated by his or her credit limit.

Payoff Rate: For deferred interest products, the payoff rate is the percentage of the total deferred interest products in which the full balance is repaid prior to the end of the deferred interest period divided by the total number of deferred interest products originated.

Penalty APR: The APR charged on existing balances and new transactions if a consumer triggers the penalty terms in his/her credit card contract. Potential triggers include making late payments, going over one's credit limit, or having one's check returned. These rates usually are higher than the standard or introductory rates. Under the CARD Act, if a consumer becomes more than sixty days late, the penalty APR may be applied to his/her existing balance.

Penalty Fee: Fees charged if a consumer violates the terms of his/her cardholder agreement or other requirements related to the account. Examples of violations include making late payments or going over one's credit limit.

Pre-Approved Offer: Mail solicitation sent by issuers to consumers that issuers have pre- screened for creditworthiness and who, based upon the evidence reviewed, are qualified to receive a credit card.

Prime: The subset of FICO scores between 660 and 719. VantageScore 801- 900 = B or Prime Plus, and 701-800 = C or Prime.

Private Label Credit Card: Credit cards issued and/or managed by a financial institution on behalf of a merchant or a wholesale manufacturer for use only in that merchant establishment.

Prudential Regulators: The collection of regulators charged with monitoring the safety and soundness of the financial system (including the Federal Reserve Board, FDIC, OCC, and NCUA).

Regulation Z: The implementing regulation for the Truth in Lending Act.

Repricing: A practice in which an issuer changes a consumer's APR.

Revolver: Consumer that carries a balance on a credit card from one billing cycle to another without paying the full amount of the balance. For purposes of this report, revolvers are consumers who are required to make a payment but do not pay their balance in full for two consecutive months. For purposes of this report, there can be revolvers that pay their balance in full in a single month.

RFI: Request for Information.

Risk Based Pricing: The practice in which an issuer extends credit with different pricing terms based on the underlying risk associated with a particular customer.

Risk Score: A score which provides a relative ranking of risk for a given consumer. Two leading risk scores are provided by Fair Isaac Corporation (FICO) and by VantageScore, a joint venture by three credit reporting agencies (Equifax, TransUnion, Experian).

Safe Harbor: A provision of a statute or a regulation that specifies that certain conduct will be deemed not to violate a given rule.

Small Business Credit Card: A credit card issued to small business owners.

Subprime: The subset of FICO scores below 660, inclusive of both Core Subprime and Deep Subprime scores; VantageScore 601-700 = D or Non-Prime, and 501-600 = F or High Risk.

Superprime: The subset of FICO scores 720 and above; VantageScore 901-990 =A or Super Prime.

TILA: Truth in Lending Act

Total Cost of Credit ("TCC"): The total cost paid by consumers, including annual fees, interest charges as well as penalty fees, calculated for a period of time and annualized and presented as a percentage of average balance over the same period of time.

Transactor: A cardholder that pays in full in each cycle and does not carry a balance from month to month. For purposes of calculation in this report, transactors are accounts that pay their balances in full for two consecutive cycles. For purposes of this report, there are accounts that pay their balances in full in a single month and are still not considered to be transactors.

UDAP: Unfair and Deceptive Acts and Practices

Unused Line: The difference between the consumer's credit line and the balance on the account at any given point in time.

Vantagescore: A set of widely used risk scores developed by credit reporting agencies to assess a consumer's creditworthiness. VantageScores can range from 501 to 990 (though in 2013, a new VantageScore scale was introduced that ranges from 300 to 850). The VantageScore scale can be mapped to letter grades from A to F, where F represents the highest risk of default. The score range translates to letter grades as follows: 901-990 = A (Super Prime), 801- 900 = B (Prime Plus), 701-800 = C (Prime), 601-700 = D (Non-Prime), and 501-600 = F (High Risk).

Yield: Total return over a period of time as a percentage of average total balances over that same period of time.

End Notes

[1] Pub. L. No. 111-24, 123 Stat. 1734 (2009).

[2] Letter from Lauren K. Saunders, Attorney, Nat'l. Consumer Law Center, to Christopher Dodd, Chairman Committee on Banking and Housing and Urban Affairs and Richard Shelby,

Senator (May 23, 2002), *available at* http://www.nclc.org/images/pdf/credit_cards/doddsupportletter0309.pdf; *Comments from the National Consumer Law Center et. al to the Consumer Financial Protection Bureau, Docket No. R- 1370 (Nov. 20, 2009) available at* http://www.nclc.org/images/pdf/credit_cards/card-regulationsto- fed1109.pdf; Comments from the Center for Responsible Lending, to the Consumer Financial Protection Bureau, Docket No. CFPB-2012-0048 (Feb. 19, 2013) *available at* http://www.responsiblelending.org/credit-cards/policy-legislation/regulators/credit-card-comment- final2-19-2013.pdf

[3] U.S. Consumer Fin. Prot. Bureau, *CFPB Bulletin 2012-06, Marketing of Credit Card Add-On Products* (July 18, 2012), http://files.consumerfinance.gov/f/201207_cfpb_bulletin_marketing_of_credit_card_addon_products. pdf (last visited on September 20, 2013).

[4] Pub. L. No. 111-24, § 2, 123 Stat. 1734, 1735 (2009)

[5] 12 U.S.C. § 5581(b)(1) (2012).

[6] *See id.* § 1616(a).

[7] *See id.* § 1616(c)(2).

[8] The Board initially implemented the CARD Act in stages with three rulemakings. *See* 75 Fed. Reg. 36077 (July 22, 2009); 75 Fed. Reg. 7658 (Feb. 22, 2010); 75 Fed. Reg. 37526 (June 29, 2010). The Board subsequently made changes to the rules in April 25, 2011. 76 Fed. Reg. 22948 (Apr. 25, 2011).

[9] 15 U.S.C. § 1601 *et seq.*

[10] Historically, Regulation Z of the Board, 12 C.F.R Part 226 (2013), has implemented TILA. The Dodd- Frank Act, Pub. L. 111–203,124 Stat. 1376 (2010), amended a number of consumer financial protection laws, including TILA. In addition to various substantive amendments, the Dodd-Frank Act generally transferred rulemaking authority for TILA to the Bureau, effective July 21, 2011. *See* Dodd-Frank Act §§1061, 1100A. Pursuant to the Dodd-Frank Act and TILA, as amended, the Bureau published an interim final rule recodifying Regulation Z (Truth in Lending), 12 C.F.R Part 1026, implementing TILA (except with respect to persons excluded from the Bureau's rulemaking authority by section 1029 of the Dodd-Frank Act).

[11] 74 Fed. Reg. 5498 (Jan. 29, 2009).

[12] Pub. L. 111-24, 123 Stat. 1734 (2009).

[13] See 75 Fed. Reg. 36077 (July 22, 2009); 75 Fed. Reg. 7658 (Feb. 22, 2010); 75 Fed. Reg. 37526 (June 29, 2010); 76 Fed. Reg. 22948 (Apr. 25, 2011).

[14] 76 Fed. Reg. 79768 (Dec. 22, 2011); 12 CFR Part 1026 (2013).

[15] 15 U.S.C. §§ 1637(i)(1), 1666i-1(b)(4), 1666i-2(a), 1665c (2012); *see also* 12 C.F.R. §§ 1026.55, 59 (2013).

[16] 15 U.S.C. § 1665d (2012); 12 C.F.R. § 1026.52(b)(1)(ii) (2013).

[17] The Bureau shall calculate each year price level adjusted amounts using the Consumer Price Index in effect on June 1 of that year. When the cumulative change in the adjusted minimum value derived from applying the annual Consumer Price level to the current amounts has risen by a whole dollar, those amounts will be increased by $1.00. 12 C.F.R. pt. 1026 Commentary 52(b)(1)(ii)-2 (2013).

[18] 15 U.S.C. § 1637(k) (2012); *see also* 12 C.F.R. § 1026.56 (2013).

[19] 15 U.S.C. § 1637(n) (2012); 12 C.F.R. § 1026.52(a) (2013).

[20] In March 2013, the Bureau finalized a revision to a 2011 rule that the Board had issued on credit card fees (78 Fed. Reg. 18795, 18796 (Mar. 28, 2013)). The final rule was in response to a federal court ruling in 2012 that granted a preliminary injunction to block a part of the Board's 2011 rule from taking effect. The Board's 2010 implementing regulation limited certain fees charged during the first year after the account is opened to 25 percent of the account's initial credit limit. In April, 2011, the Board revised the implementing regulation to expand the fee limitation to fees that consumers were required to pay *prior* to account opening (76 Fed. Reg. 22948 (Apr. 25, 2011)). A lawsuit alleged that the Board had exceeded its authority by expanding the rule to apply to fees a consumer is required to pay prior to account opening (*See* First Premier Bank v. U.S. Consumer Fin. Prot. Bureau, 819

F. Supp. 2d. 906, 923 (D.S.D. Sept. 23, 2011)). The Bureau's final rule provided that the 25 percent limitation does not apply to fees paid prior to account opening.

[21] 15 U.S.C. §§ 1637(b)(12)(C), (o); 1666b(a); 1666c(a),(c) (2012); 12 C.F.R. §§ 1026.5(b)(2)(ii), .7(b)(11)(i)(A), .10(b)(2)(ii), .10(b)(3), .10(d), .10(f) (2013).

[22] 15 U.S.C. § 1666c(b) (2012); *see also* 12 C.F.R. § 1026.53 (2013).

[23] 15 U.S.C § 1637(b)(11), (12) (2012); *see also* 12 C.F.R. § 1026.7(b)(11)-(13) (2013).

[24] 15 U.S.C. § 1665e (2012); *see also* 12 C.F.R. § 1026.51(a) (2013); 12 C.F.R. pt. 1026 Commentary 51(a)(1)(i)-5.iv (2013).

[25] 15 U.S.C. §§ 1637(c)(8), 1650(f)(2), 1681b(c)(1)(B)(iv) (2012); *see also* 12 C.F.R. §§ 1026.51(b), 57 (2013).

[26] *See* 77 Fed. Reg. 75410-01 (Dec 20, 2012).

[27] Request for Information Regarding Credit Card Market (CFPB-2012-0048), *available at* http://www.regulations.gov/#!docketBrowser;rpp=25;po=0;dct=PS;D=CFPB-2012-0048

[28] For more information on scoring models, please refer to the Consumer Fin. Prot. Bureau, *Analysis of Differences between Consumer- and Credit-Purchased Credit Scores* (Sep. 2012), *available at* http://files.consumerfinance.gov/f/201209_Analysis_Differences _Consumer_Credit.pdf

[29] FICO Banking Analytics Blog, FICO Score Distribution Remains Mixed (Apr. 15, 2013), *available at* http://bankinganalyticsblog.. fico.com/2013/04/fico-score-distribution-remains-mixed.. html

[30] National Bureau of Economic Research, US Business Cycle Expansions and Contractions (Sep. 19, 2010), *available at* http://www.nber.org/cycles.html

[31] St. Louis Federal Reserve Bank, Monthly Unemployment Series, *available at* http://research.stlouisfed.org/fred2/graph/?s[1][id]=UNEMPLOY

[32] Moody's Analytics, Credit Card Charge-Off Excel Data Supplement (12/2007 & 6/2009).

[33] 75 Fed. Reg. 7658 (Feb. 22, 2010)

[34] 15 U.S.C. § 1616(a)(4)(A) (2012).

[35] General Accounting Office, *Credit Cards: Increased Complexity in Rates and Fees Heightens Need for More Effective Disclosures to Consumers (2006).*

[36] 15 U.S.C. § 1637(k) (2012).

[37] 15 U.S.C. § 1637(k) (2012).

[38] 15 U.S.C. § 1665d(a) (2012).

[39] 12 C.F.R. § 1026.52(b)(1)(ii) (2013).

[40] General Accounting Office, *Credit Cards: Increased Complexity in Rates and Fees Heightens Need for More Effective Disclosures to Consumers (2006).*

[41] Comments from the National Consumer Law Center et. al to the Consumer Financial Protection Bureau, Docket No. R-1384 (Apr. 14, 2010) *available at* http://www.nclc.org/ images/pdf/credit_cards/comments-frb-card-4-14-10.pdf

[42] 15 U.S.C. § 1637(o)(2) (2012). The Card Act also requires that payments on a credit card made in person at a branch or office of a card issuer that is a financial institution prior to the close of business of that branch or office must be considered received on the date on which the consumer makes the payment. *See* 15 U.S.C. § 1637(b)(12)(C) (2012). In addition, pursuant to the Card Act, the implementing regulations provide that issuers may not set cut-off times for payments to be received earlier than 5 p.m. on the payment due date at the location specified by the creditor for the receipt of such payments. See 15 U.S.C. § 1666c(a) (2012); 12 C.F.R. § 1026.10(b)(2)(ii) (2013). Moreover, if a card issuer makes a material change to the address for receiving payment or procedures for receiving payments and such change causes a material delay in the crediting of a payment to the consumer account during the 60-day period following the date on which such change took effect, the card issuer may not impose any late fee or interest charge for a late payment on the card account during the 60-day period following the date on which the change took effect. 15 U.S.C. § 1666c(c) (2012).

[43] 15 U.S.C. §§ 1637(o)(1), 1666b(a), 1637(b)(12) (2012), respectively.

[44] 15 U.S.C. § 1665d(a) (2012).

[45] 12 C.F.R. § 1026.52(b)(1)(ii) (2013).
[46] 15 U.S.C. § 1666i-1 (2012).
[47] 15 U.S.C. §§ 1637(i), 1665c(b) (2012).
[48] 73 Fed. Reg. 28904 (May 19, 2008).
[49] 15 U.S.C. § 1681b(c)(1)(B)(iv) (2012).
[50] The CFPB amended Regulation Z to remove the requirement that issuers consider the consumer's independent ability to pay for consumers who are 21 or older, and permits issuers to consider income and assets to which such consumers have a reasonable expectation of access for consumers who are 21 or older. *See* 12 C.F.R. § 1026.51(a) (2013).
[51] 15 U.S.C. § 1637(c)(8) (2012).
[52] 15 U.S.C. § 1650(f)(2) (2012).
[53] *Id.* at § 1665e; 12 C.F.R. § 1026.51(a) (2013).
[54] 78 Fed. Reg. 25818 (May 3, 2013).
[55] 15 U.S.C. § 1637(c)(8) (2012).
[56] Bank of America Corp., Annual Report (Form 10-K), 61 (Dec. 31, 2009), http://www.sec.gov/ Archives/edgar/data/70858/000119312510041666/d10k.htm.
[57] Bank of America Corp., Annual Report (Form 10-K), 106, (Dec. 31, 2009), http://www. sec.gov/ Archives/edgar/data/70858/000119312510041666/d10k.htm.
[58] 15 U.S.C. § 1637(b)(11), (12) (2012).
[59] 15 U.S.C. § 1666c(b) (2012).
[60] *See* 12 C.F.R. § 1026.6(b)(1) and (2) (2013).
[61] 15 U.S.C. § 1637(b)(11), (12) (2012).
[62] 15 U.S.C. § 1637(b)(11), (12) (2012).
[63] 12 C.F.R. § 1026.7(b)(12)(F) (2013).
[64] 12 C.F.R. § 1026 App.G (2013).
[65] 15 U.S.C. § 1665c (2012).
[66] 15 U.S.C. § 1661 (2012).
[67] Melody Warrick, *10 ways to get more from your credit card through social media*, http://www.creditcards.com/credit-card-news/10-ways-use-credit_card-social_media-1273.php (last visited on September 19, 2013).
[68] Fed. Reserve Bd., *Consumer and Mobile Financial Services 2013* (March 2013), *available at* http://www.federalreserve.gov/econresdata/consumers-and-mobile-financial-services-report- 201303.pdf.
[69] Sarah Todd & Chris Cummings, *The Clear Reason Why These Card Issuers Are On Top*, Am. Banker, August 22, 2013, at page 1, *available at* http://www.americanbanker. com/issues/178_162/the-clear- reason-why-these-card-issuers-are-on-top-1061496-1.html? zkPrintable=tue; Press Release, J.D. Power, *2013 US Credit Card Satisfaction Study* (Aug. 22, 2013), *available at* http://www.jdpower.com/content/ press-release/KrslSk2/2013-u-s-credit-card-satisfaction-study.htm; *Card Hub, , 2013 Credit Card Application Study* (2013), http://www.cardhub.com/edu/credit-card- application-study-2013/ (last visited on September 19, 2013).
[70] J.D. Power, *2013 US Credit Card Satisfaction Study* (Aug. 22, 2013), *available at* http://www.jdpower.com/content/press-release/KrslSk2/2013-u-s-credit-card-satisfaction-study.htm.
[71] J.D. Power, *2013 US Credit Card Satisfaction Study* (Aug. 22, 2013), *available at* http://www.jdpower.com/content/press-release/KrslSk2/2013-u-s-credit-card-satisfaction-study.htm.
[72] 75 Fed. Reg. 58539 (Sept. 24, 2010).
[73] Press Release, U.S. Consumer Fin. Prot. Bureau, *Federal Deposit Insurance Corporation and Consumer Financial Protection Bureau Order Discover to Pay $200 Million Consumer Refund for Deceptive Marketing*, http://www.consumerfinance.gov/pressreleases/discover-consent-order/ (last visited on September 20, 2013); Press Release, U.S. Consumer Fin.

Prot. Bureau, *CFPB Probe into Capital One Credit Card Marketing Results in $140 Million Consumer Refund*, http://www.consumerfinance.gov/pressreleases/cfpb-capital-one-probe/ (last visited on September 20, 2013); Press Release, U.S. Consumer Fin. Prot. Bureau, *CFPB Orders Chase and JPMorgan Chase to Pay $309 Million Refund for Illegal Credit Card Practices* (Sep. 19, 2013), http://www.consumerfinance.gov/newsroom/cfpb-orders-chase-and-jpmorgan-chase-to-pay-309- million-refund-for-illegal-credit-card-practices/ (last visited on September 20, 2013).

[74] U.S. Consumer Fin. Prot. Bureau, *CFPB Bulletin 2012-06, Marketing of Credit Card Add-On Products* (July 18, 2012), http://files.consumerfinance.gov/f/201207_cfpb_bulletin_marketing_of_credit_card_addon_products. pdf (last visited on September 20, 2013).

[75] *Fed. Trade Comm'n v. CompuCredit Corp.*, Fed. Trade Comm'n File No.: 062-3212, Case No. 1:08CV01976, (N.D. Ga. Dec. 19, 2008), *available at* http://www.ftc.gov/os/caselist/0623212/index.shtm.

[76] *See* 15 U.S.C. § 1637(n) (2012); 75 Fed. Reg. 7658 (Feb. 22, 2010); 12 C.F.R. 1026.52(a) (2013).

[77] 76 Fed. Reg. 22948 (Apr. 25, 2011).

[78] *See id.* at 22977.

[79] *See First Premier Bank v. U.S. Consumer Fin. Prot. Bureau*, 819 F. Supp. 2d906, 923. (D.S.D. 2011).

[80] 78 Fed. Reg. 18795, 18796 (Mar. 28, 2013).

[81] 78 Fed. Reg. 18795, 18796 (Mar. 28, 2013).

[82] *See id.*

[83] *Id.*

[84] *Id.* at 18796.

[85] See 74 F.R. 5498 (Jan. 29, 2009), 75 FR 7925 (Feb. 22, 2010).

[86] 15 U.S.C. §§ 1637(n)(2) (2012).

[87] 15 U.S.C. § 1666c(b)(2) (2012);15 U.S.C. § 1666 i-2(b) (2012).

[88] 75 Fed. Reg. 7658 (Feb. 22, 2010).

[89] 12 C.F.R.§ 1026.55(b)(1) (2013).

[90] *Id.* at 1026.16(h).

[91] 12 C.F.R. pt. 1026, Commentary 7(b)-1. (2013).

[92] 12 C.F.R. §§ 1026.7(b)(14), app. G (2013).

[93] 12 C.F.R. § 1026.53(b)(1)(ii) (2013).

[94] Mercator Advisory Group fielded this online (web-based) survey between May 19-24, 2011, using the U.S. online consumer research panel managed by the research firm TNS. A total of 1,012 responses were obtained from adults age 18 and over. Other than the age qualification, no additional respondent screening was conducted, as the sampling objective was to obtain a broad profile reflective of U.S. consumer households. In general, samples of this size have a sampling error of +/- 3.1% at the 95% confidence level for questions reported for all respondents (sub-segment analyses have higher sampling errors due to the reduced sub-sample size).

[95] Mercator Advisory Services Grp., *Credit Card Rewards Program: Balancing Loyalty and Profitability* 7 (2013).

[96] *Id.* at 8.

[97] The 2013 Credit Card Satisfaction Study includes responses from more than 14,000 credit card customers and was fielded from May through June 2013.

[98] J.D. Power, *2013 US Credit Card Satisfaction Study* (Aug. 22, 2013), *available at* http://www.jdpower.com/content/press-release/KrslSk2/2013-u-s-credit-card-satisfaction-study.htm.

[99] *Id.*

Index

L

M

N

O

P

R